D1572011

VOICES *of* LGBTQ+

A Conversation Starter for Understanding, Supporting, and Protecting Gay, Bi, Trans, and Queer People

LYNDA WOLTERS

www.mascotbooks.com

VOICES *of* LGBTQ+

Cover portraits by Chris Taylor
facebook.com/chrisarttaylor
Instagram: @artistchris

Author photo on dust jacket by Taylor Humby, humbyart.com

The portraits on the cover of this book depict actual people who are part of the LGBTQ+ community. Their names are Shannon Hansen, Hunter Johnson, Elizabeth Delk, Ashley Branch, Jackson Moore, and Taylor Humby.

For more information, please contact:
Mascot Books
620 Herndon Parkway #320
Herndon, VA 20170
info@mascotbooks.com

Library of Congress Control Number: 2020902752

CPSIA Code: PRFRE0420A
ISBN-13: 978-1-64543-148-0

Printed in Canada

This book is dedicated to the people in the LGBTQ+ community and those supporting them.

CONTENTS

PREFACE

Dear Mom and Dad,

I have to tell you something. You may not like what I have to say, but it is imperative to my mental health and my emotional well-being that I say this. I am not who you think I am. I am not what you see. I have tried so hard, but I can't do it any longer; I cannot live a lie just to make you happy. I must be true to myself.

I do not *feel* the way you *see* me. I am not what I appear on the outside. Your child, perfect in creation, is not actually the way I am "supposed to be." Inside I am confused, scared, and alone. I am a member of the LGBTQ+ community.

I tried, I really did. I pushed those feelings down until I thought I would explode, or worse—kill myself. You should probably know that I have actually thought about that, sometimes going so far as to nearly putting my plan into action. But I love you, I need you, I don't want to disappoint you, so I stay around. But I am miserable, Mom, and I can't do this anymore, Dad.

Please don't hate me, don't stop loving me; I don't know how I will get through this without you. I realize this is not what you have learned in church, and I know you are going to be worried about what your friends say when they find out, but I'm still your child—your *little one*.

I've had a lot of years to figure this out, and I can assure you this isn't a passing phase. This is not going to go away with time, and no amount of prayer or conversation is going to *change me back*. This is me.

Don't give up on me; I won't give up on you. I get that you will need time to process all this—God knows I have needed time as well. You will stumble with the newness of it all, call me the wrong name or use an incorrect pronoun if I identify as transgender, or forget to refer to my significant other as my *partner* and not just my friend if I come out as gay or lesbian, or be frustrated and confused when I tell you I am queer, non-binary, or asexual.

What I am telling you will hurt you, I understand, and you may even feel guilty as if you did something wrong, or perhaps didn't do enough of something. None of that is true—this isn't about you.

I can give you some space now, and a lot of grace, as you process what you have likely known for a very long time to be true. But this will be a finite amount of time, as I can no longer live in limbo. I must come out and be my authentic self, whatever that looks like.

I love you, Mom. I love you, Dad. Please remember I am still your child and always will be, but I am also part of the LGBTQ+ community.

INTRODUCTION
Key LGBTQ+ Terms

FOR EASE OF READING, I am briefly listing a few terms used throughout this book. A more complete and concise list can be found in the glossary at the end of the book.

LGBTQ+: Acronym for lesbian, gay, bisexual, transgender and queer (queer meaning questioning, or other than what is thought of as cisgender/heteronormative). The "+" symbol is an all-inclusive sign that encompasses any other non-cisgender, non-heteronormative person; i.e., pansexual, asexual, fluid. The "+" also includes allies; i.e., those who advocate for and stand with those in the LGBTQ+ community.

Lesbian: A female who is attracted to another female.

Gay: A person sexually attracted to another of the same gender. The term "gay" can be all encompassing as anyone attracted to the same gender (as in "gay woman"); however, it is more often specific to the male gender.

Bisexual: A person who is sexually attracted to people who identify as male or female.

Straight: A person who is sexually attracted to the opposite sex; i.e., a woman attracted to a man is straight.

Gender: Either of the two sexes as defined by social and cultural difference rather than biological difference.

Transgender: A person who identifies as a gender that is different from the biological sex they were at birth; i.e., a transgender female is someone born biologically male but who identifies as female.

Cisgender: A person who identifies as the same gender as their biological sex at birth; i.e., a man who identifies as a male and was born male is "cisgender."

Heteronormative: Relating to a worldview that treats the straight sexuality of cisgender people as the "norm" or preferred behavior.

The terms "homosexual" and "heterosexual" are antiquated and have been generally replaced by "gay" and "straight." These terms are not considered slang or derogatory when used in proper context. That being said, throwing around the word "gay" or "queer" in a disparaging way is not only considered hateful, it is also rude.

During this book I focus mainly on gay, lesbian, and transgender people because there are upwards of ninety recognized sexual orientations and gender identities, and I could not give justice to them all in one book. This does not diminish or undermine any of the other smaller "categories"; I simply wanted to be consistent. However, everything I write herein relates to everyone who is a member of the wonderfully diverse LGBTQ+ community.

Note: You will notice throughout this writing there are instances where only LGB, LGBT, or LGBTQ (without the +) are used. This is intentional as those are specific to certain research or references. I have made every effort to identify correctly and be inclusive of all persons throughout, and ask for grace if there is an error; I, too, am human.

My Son, Hunter

Almost from the moment my youngest son was born, I knew he was different from his two older brothers. Obviously, his character had yet to be formed, but I had a *feeling*, a sense that he was different; I knew he was gay. I have no basis for this other than just being his mom. He didn't make a choice—he just *was*. It took him years to recognize and accept that he wasn't like anyone else he knew, and part of that was denial; he didn't *want* to be different, but he found he couldn't pretend or ignore it.

Hunter has been living an openly gay life now for ten years. Still a young man, he has a lot to say about his life and how he has been treated as a gay male in a heteronormative, cisgender world.

I have learned much from Hunter and have become a better person for him. Watching his plight for acceptance, I feel compelled to be an advocate for him and others who are LGBTQ+, which for those of you who are new to the terminology, stands for lesbian, gay, bisexual, transgender, and questioning/queer.

I will not profess to know what it is like to be gay, transgender, bisexual, or even curious, but I can see the injustice, inequality, unacceptance, and fear of, toward, and within this community. I am writing this book to be a positive conversation starter, a book that educates and dispels myths and fears for people who are coming to terms with their own sexuality or a loved one's.

Initially, I was only going to write about gay and lesbian people—the safer route for me because I had some "skin in that game" with a gay son. I thought I could easily speak with some of Hunter's friends, many of whom I already knew, get an idea of how they felt, and start writing. I also knew I would not face nearly as much backlash as I would if I wrote about the far less tolerated transgender population—a point that was brought to my attention by several people as I discussed my desire to write this book. One person even suggested I should not have the book published until after I was dead, thinking that I could then circumvent the negativity that would likely be cast my way from the religious community in particular.

Hunter, however, adamantly insisted I include the broader LGBTQ+ community, not for fear of being politically correct but, as he explained, because transgender people are unfairly marginalized and invisible to the vast majority of the populous. He said I should truly reconsider my position.

I told Hunter I knew nothing about transgender people and didn't understand their feelings of identifying as someone different than they were. I told him I would not know where to start. He smiled a little "how quickly you have forgotten" grin and reminded me that while my eldest son was not transgender, he does now iden-tify as someone different than he was growing up.

My eldest son was given the name Jordan when he was born. I chose the name, and I loved it. He spent twenty-plus years with that name, and I anticipated he would spend the rest of his life with it; I was wrong. Somewhere during his college days, he took on the pseudonym, Kowboy. I never really thought much about it, imagining it was just a passing phase or a silly nickname. But several years later, he said to me, "Momma, I hate the name Jordan. I don't use it, and I no longer identify as that person. And I really wish you wouldn't use it."

I remember going into defense mode, saying something like, "Son, that is your name. I am not going to call you by some nick-name like Kowboy."

He responded very simply, without defense or anger: "Jordan is dead to me, Momma. I don't want anything to do with him. I prefer the name Kowboy."

I was miffed but told him I would try to use his nickname. I complained to my two other sons about this new persona. I explained to Adam, my middle son, that I was fearful Jordan might disown me if I didn't call him Kowboy. Adam simply said, "That's just Jordan, Mom." He was right. Jordan had always had a preference for things being black or white, wrong or right; there was no middle ground. Adam said as weird as it felt to us to use a different name for Jordan, we should respect him and do our best.

When I spoke with Hunter about this, hoping to get at least one of my kids on my side, he intuitively and matter-of-factly said to me, "Mom, it's just like a transgender person."

"What?" I yelled through the phone. "He's not transgender!"

"No, Mom, but transgender people also use a new name when they finally come out. When they identify as the different gender, they pick a name that suits that sex and who they are. Their given name, or birth name, becomes their 'dead' name. All Jordan is telling you is he has identified with a new part of himself and the old part, the part we know as Jordan, is dead. He doesn't want anything to do with the old Jordan, so to him, the name Jordan is a reminder, an insult—it's disrespectful."

Hunter went on to remind me that Jordan's past was riddled with events Kowboy would rather not remember. Jordan was in a very bad spot for several years and had finally found himself again. He had become someone he could respect and like, and he attached a new identity to it; hence, Kowboy was born and Jordan was dead.

In my wildest dreams, I would never have come to terms with this Kowboy identity had Hunter not explained it in transgender terminology. It was like a light bulb came on for me. Jordan wasn't trying to disrespect me by changing his name or identifying as someone different. In fact, "Kowboy" had absolutely nothing to do with me and everything to do with my beautiful son, who had seen so much tragedy and pain and simply wanted never to be reminded of or associated with those days again.

As a mother who has these "differences" within her own family, I understand how hard it is to know what to say or what not to say, what is politically correct, and what is offensive. I just do my best. I try to be as open and honest as I can without disrespecting my kids. And I understand that *I don't have to understand everything*—but I need to accept my children as they are and where they are. I try to lead with love and kindness and acceptance. Differences in people can lead to fear in others, which can cause hatred, animosity, aggression, and violence. Therefore, I hope to encourage open dialogue and honest communication through this book.

Despite my personal experiences, research and conversations, I still don't have all the answers, but I am learning and I am trying. I think that is the least any of us should do. I have found through talking with people who identify as LGBTQ+ that they have the same core desires as anyone: to be able to live their lives in peace and without fear, and to be treated fairly and equally. I also found I had many other things in common with these people—their family connections, love of their children, their faith, careers, pets, hobbies, volunteer activities, and vacations. I learned we share the same worries about finances, concerns over their children's education, and fear of their kids being bullied. We have the same hopes about world peace, uneasiness about politics and the economy. What I learned was humans are all alike.

To write this book, I had conversations with several people from all walks of diversity: gay, lesbian, bisexual, and transgender. I have taken their thoughts, ideas, suggestions, fears, hopes, and humor and given them a platform to tell those who do not wear their shoes what it feels like to walk a mile in them.

Ironically, this book ended up leaning heavily toward the transgender population, the ultra-marginalized subgroup I had not wanted to initially cover. But through my own education, I realized the need for their voices to not just be heard, but to be louder than the others—they endure so much hate, so much misunderstanding. I found it fascinating that gay and lesbian people all mentioned how grateful they were that the challenges they faced only related to their sexuality, not their gender. Some even went so far as to tell me they pray their own children don't "turn out to be trans."

Equally fascinating to me was learning that there is a social order within the LGBTQ+ community. Lesbians and bisexual women are perceived to be at the highest point in the community with "lipstick lesbians"—the term for "conventionally beautiful" women—being the pinnacle of them all. The "macho gays" who can "pass" as straight and who often have a fear of men who are considered "too gay," are the next on the ladder, with the rest of the gay men on the lower rungs. Interestingly enough, it is considered sexy by most to be a bisexual woman, yet it is almost disrespectful to gay males if you are a bisexual male. Lower down the pecking order are the mishmash of bisexual men, queer and questioning, and asexual people, who are often overlooked as a subcategory and not even considered to be within the LGBTQ+ community. And then there is the transgender community. Any way you slice it, they are at the bottom of their own community; and they know it. But they too have an intercommunity order of acceptance: those having both top and bottom Gender Confirmation Surgery (GCS) are at the top, people who have had only top surgery (either the implantation of breasts or the removal of natural breasts) are in the middle of the order, but those who have had no surgeries fall to the lowest level—they apparently are not transgender *enough*.

I am not attempting to cover every aspect of the lives of LGBTQ+ individuals, nor is this book a reflection of every scenario or example of what is faced by members of the LGBTQ+ community; everyone's story is different. It is only a snapshot, an overview of their difficulties, which will serve to highlight our need to change and accept all people as human beings worthy of equal treatment, kindness, and love.

Voices of LGBTQ+ is merely a starting point for education and conversation. A place where loved ones and friends can turn to gather some basic insight into why this group of people feel persecuted and what we can do to help change that. And, hopefully, *Voices of LGBTQ+* can also dispel some misconceptions that the LGBTQ+ community is trying to gain *different* or *additional* rights and equalities than anyone else, which simply is not true. This, however, has become a common misconception and excuse for not enacting anti-discrimination policies on their behalf.

My wish is to show that we can still have our politics and our religion as well as our gay, lesbian, transgender, and queer friends, and family.

CHAPTER 1

Naturally Different

BEING THE YOUNGEST IN THE family wasn't always easy for Hunter. Growing up, my three boys loved each other the way siblings do, but they argued, called each other names, got into a lot of mischief, and threw a few punches, some of which I learned about years after they were grown. Kowboy and Adam, my two other sons, always had a sense that Hunter was different from them, and sometimes they threw this in his face. The older boys were not any meaner to Hunter than they were to each other. But occasionally they would call him disparaging names they had heard used to put someone down. And when they did—look out! I was all over that.

All three of my boys went through a phase when they let the little girl who lived up the street paint their toenails and fingernails. Did that *make* them gay or transgender? No. It made them kids having fun doing what kids do, experimenting with Mom's makeup. And experiment they did. They all went through an eyeliner phase, and I am pretty sure I remember some full-on face painting with the boys coming out of the bathroom, hands on hips, wearing my bright red lipstick, their hair in clips, and wobbling atop my high-heeled shoes. "Aren't we pretty?" they would giggle and laugh, poking fun at themselves and me. Were they all going to be transvestites or transgender? No. None of them—they were just kids being silly.

While all three boys would get goofy with dying their hair (which they did for years, every color from bright orange to green, blue, and blond), Hunter was the one who would comment to me several times about how girls had more fun by being able to wear makeup and wear a wide variety of clothes. "All we have is pants!" Hunter would say. And at eight years old, which of my sons asked for an Easy Bake Oven—specifically, a *pink* Easy Bake Oven? Hunter, of course. I didn't care that he asked for this, and I didn't care what color he wanted: he got exactly what he asked for. It certainly didn't stigmatize him as being gay or transgender, but his brothers were quick to recognize what had already been socially instilled in them. They hurled insults over the pink Easy Bake Oven, saying, "You're so gay!"

"DO NOT EVER call your brother that," I would tell them, wanting to defend Hunter from these types of attacks. We all knew he was different and assumed he was gay; we talked about it often when he wasn't around, as the other two boys had questions. But Hunter had not yet figured it out, and I felt that no one, not even his brothers or I, had the right to bully him or label him.

Hunter's brothers grew up to be two of his biggest supporters and protectors regarding his sexual orientation. As adults, they both adamantly defend him and his rights as a human and would, I dare say, lay anything down for him. But how did it feel for Hunter to come out, to figure out he was gay, to acknowledge it, to be brave enough to face his brothers, Mom, Dad, and friends? Surely he must have worried about whether he would be accepted or shunned.

As his mother, I have always felt protective of him, as any parent does their child, but I realized not long ago that I had never really *had his back*, other than in our very immediate family. By very immediate, I mean his brothers and his father—but not *my* father, Hunter's grandfather. I never had the strength or the courage to address my son's sexual orientation with my own dad. In fact, I actually encouraged Hunter to avoid the topic. "It's just easier that way," I explained to him.

I did not realize until recently that while I was proud to defend my son against any insults from his brothers, I was hiding behind my own walls regarding everyone else. I was never ashamed of my son—far from it, I am extremely proud of him as a person and as my son—but I was too concerned with what others, particularly my father, might say if I stood up against the social norm and defended my child in any way that might draw negative attention to me and my family in the eyes of society.

My father was an active, highly visible, and incredibly well-known man at our state's capitol. For seventeen years, he was present at that beautifully ornate building that created Idaho's state laws and molded its future. My dad was *someone* in his own right, and I was afraid to stand up to him about my son's "difference," as it might hamper his standing, which in turn would have meant disrespect from me. This was simply not done in my family.

In our state, legislation has never been passed that would ensure equality and anti-discrimination rights of the LGBTQ+ community. This proposed legislation is referred to as "Add the Words," referring to four words: *sexual orientation* and *gender identity*. These simple words would mean laws and protection against discrimination for gay and transgender people. Advocates for this legislation would often line the halls of the capitol and the steps leading up to its doors with their hands over their mouths in silent protest as a way to show their support for the community. Meanwhile, people like my dad would be behind closed doors helping determine the fate of people who are LGBTQ+. And while the supporters were mostly peaceful, they were often arrested for petty indiscretions during their rallies.

My dad, however, did not keep silent. He was actually video-taped becoming defiant, nearly belligerent, against these protestors for blocking a door so he and others could not exit, regardless of the numerous other doors available to all. Would my dad be arrested? Would he be held accountable for his insults, his disparaging words, and near-threats? No. He would be called to testify as a prosecution witness against the silent protesters for blocking the door. My dad was seemingly a hero to the many other extremely conservative, mostly very wealthy, seemingly all straight, older white men.

In many ways my dad was my hero also, so how could I stand up to him? How could I risk potentially losing his love by outing my son and then protecting him for it? I couldn't, and I didn't. My dad passed away with the rest of us keeping Hunter's sexual orientation secret.

In addition to completely letting my child down, I also took away my dad's ability to answer for himself. In all honesty, I have no idea how he would have behaved; I never gave him the opportunity to show me. Sure, I can surmise all day long about how I think it would have all gone down, but I would be a liar to claim that I knew.

Hunter and I have talked about this, and in his usual carefree, love-all-people kind of way, he holds no animosity about this. In fact, he told me he was scared to let Grandpa know he was gay, so he completely understood my decision. Hunter and his grandpa shared a unique bond because Hunter was born on his grandpa's fifty-first birthday. They celebrated each birthday together with a joint party for the next twenty-two years, and Hunter held a very special place in his grandpa's heart for being the "most special birthday present," as my dad referred to him on the day Hunter was born. Hunter never wanted to lose that place in his grandpa's heart, and I get it. But as his mom, my heart sinks at the regret I will always have to live with.

I share this information about the relationship Hunter had with my dad because their close relationship was not enough to make any of us feel certain my dad would have reacted well to learning of Hunter's *secret*. I tell the story now because perhaps it will help you if you feel you are caught in a similarly difficult situation. You are not alone as a parent, a friend, or a coworker because when someone comes out, we do not know how others will behave, nor do we know the right thing to do. And believe me: you will make mistakes, just as I have.

After my dad's passing, I felt my biggest stumbling block had been removed, and I have become a more vocal advocate for my son regarding his human rights. It was several years after Hunter came out as gay that my oldest declared his birth name "dead" and began to identify as Kowboy. This was hard for me, but with Hunter's help in understanding how Jordan—the identity and the name—was "dead" and Kowboy was now my son, I made a real effort to support him.

How could I deny Kowboy his request for a new identity? How could I force my preference for the name I picked for him if it was going to damage him? What was I really going to do if Jordan continued to use the name Kowboy? Disown him? Kick him out of my house and my life? No. Why would any parent want to turn their child out or psychologically harm them?

I love my son, unconditionally. I loved him through the bad times. I never once turned him away, no matter what he had been through. I told him and his brothers, all their lives, "There is nothing you could ever do that would stop me from loving you." So, why was I going to let the name Kowboy stand in the way of that love? I wasn't. And I realized that most of my resistance was my assumption that I had the right to decide what his name should be. Some cultures wait until their children earn a reputation before holding a naming ceremony and declaring their true name. This isn't common in Western society, of course, but I can see the freedom this gives to young people, to make their own way and forge their own character.

I refer to my son now as Kowboy, and I correct those around me who call him by his dead name. Honestly, I miss both the name and the little boy attached to the name, but I love the man Kowboy has become, and I respect him enough to call him by his chosen name. It really isn't that hard to do.

Do I slip up? Sure, sometimes. It is even awkward at times. It is like I have to explain his "coming out" every time I talk about him to an old friend or distant relative and refer to him as Kowboy. I used to go into a long, drawn-out dissertation about how the name came about and why it is spelled with a "K" (which I really don't know, and I really don't care), and I used to sort of apologize for the change in name, like it was an embarrassment to me.

I no longer apologize. It isn't silly to my son, so it isn't silly to me. I am not embarrassed by my son, and I stand up proud when I say his name. Yes, it has taken a while, and I had to make some minor personal adjustments to ensure I don't accidentally call him Jordan (like changing his name in my phone to Kowboy). When I look back to when Jordan was born and I held that tiny baby in my arms, the name Jordan sounded just as foreign to me in those first few days as Kowboy does now. I got used to his old name, and I will get used to his new one. It is, after all, just a name.

As a parent, it is difficult to have a child who is "different" than those of my friends. I only have a few friends with gay children and none with transgender children; therefore, only a few understand when I talk about Hunter and his partner and none understand when I speak about Kowboy's new identity. That is not easy for me, and at times I feel alone with my thoughts and feelings.

We all dream of the lives our children will lead, the awards they will win, the prestige they will garner from the acclaimed university they will attend, and the boatloads of money they will make when they marry their high school (straight, cisgender) sweetheart with whom they will have 2.5 children. But that is not the reality for many of us who have skeletons (i.e., LGBTQ+ kids) in the closet—children who are dying to come out and be acknowledged.

My biggest fear raising my children and watching their strife as they became young men was that one of them may become so distraught about something that they would feel the only way out was to take their own life. I saw in Hunter's eyes, and I have seen it in Kowboy's eyes, a look that conveys their desperation to be heard and understood, loved without judgment, and accepted for their authentic selves. I would do anything to save a child, as most people would do, and the one thing I could do was navigate the unknown and find acceptance.

CHAPTER 2
LGBTQ+: Past & Present

SEXUALITY AND SEXUAL ORIENTATION HAVE been topics of interest since the beginning of time. The straight, gay, and transgender identities of people have been depicted throughout history, and representations are found in ancient Egyptian hieroglyphs, tales of Greek Gods, and paintings of the Renaissance period.

Recently, archeologists unearthed the remains of a man who is thought to have lived between 2900 and 2500 B.C. This male skeleton was found interred in a ritualistic way reserved for females, but the archeologists claim that people of this period and culture took funeral rites very seriously, so the manner of burial is not believed to be a mistake. It's more likely, they think that this was a man who was transsexual or was gay.

Ancient history has recorded gay and transgender people as being celebrated and revered in upper-class society. Transgender priestesses lived in the Mesopotamia Era, and Antinous, touted as the beautiful gay lover of Hadrian, emperor of ancient Rome, was deified and worshiped as a god.

The positive acceptance of transgender and same-sex relationships has, however, been left to our ancestors of generations and millennia ago. The horrors and atrocities faced by the LGBTQ+ community in the nineteenth, twentieth, and twenty-first centuries are not only a travesty but proof that society does not always move forward; sometimes they remain stagnant or regress.

Sadly, modern society no longer elevates this diverse culture and, instead, has often taken steps to either "fix" them or eradicate them. This group of people is perceived as different from the social norm, so they often hide their true identity in order to feel safe and sometimes in order to save their own lives.

Atrocities in Recent History

MORE THAN 100,000 KNOWN OR presumed gay men in Nazi Germany were arrested and interned in concentration camps solely because of their sexual orientation. It was not until 1994 that the law enshrined in Paragraph 175 of the German Criminal Code, which prohibited "criminally indecent activities between men," was repealed. It took another eight years for the German government to annul the convictions of "homosexual" men who were persecuted decades prior under Nazi rule. Unfortunately, most of those annulments were posthumous. Many of those gay men died at the hands of the Nazis or had passed away of natural causes by the time they were pardoned.

Interestingly, gay women were not criminalized in Germany, as lesbianism was generally viewed as less threatening to social or political order. According to Nazi ideology, lesbian women could still perform their "primary" role, which was to be "a mother of as many 'Aryan' babies as possible."[1]

As an alternative to the concentration camp, gay males during this period were sometimes given an option of castration, which was thought to ensure the so-called offenders would "never experience the same, deviant urges again." It has been mentioned that castration by way of boiling water was sometimes the method used.

Within the confines of the concentration camps, experiments were performed on so-called homosexuals (a former medical term) to try to reverse their gay tendencies or "cure" their "disease." These experiments included the implantation of synthetic hormones into their bellies, the design of which was to alter sexual urges. Everyone subjected to that experiment died.

As barbaric and unthinkable as the Nazi experiments were, news has emerged that gay "concentration camps" still exist today in the Chechen Republic, a federal subject of Russia. The first reports of these recent horrors involving the abuse to gays emerged in 2012, when vigilante groups would lure gay men, often through gay websites, then kidnap and torture them on camera and post the videos. Since then, *Novoya Gazeta,* a Russian newspaper well known for its critical investigations into Russian political and social affairs, reported that the police are often the perpetrators of the abuse, which includes electrocution, solitary confinement, beatings, dunking in vats of cold water, and starvation. The Russian LGBTQ+ Network states it has been working to evacuate people from the Chechen camps, while President Razman Kadyrov says the allegations are "absolute lies and disinformation."[2, 3]

These men are either tortured because they are gay or forced to give up the names of other gay men. Several of these men have been killed as a result of the torture and beatings, and others have been released to their families with instructions to kill their gay loved one as an "honor killing."

Matt Baume wrote an article for the site *Them*. In that article, he wrote of the continued atrocities to the LGBTQ+ community in Chechnya. When pressed on the subject, the Russian justice minister continued his claims that their investigation into allegations of a gay purge "showed that there were not any such incidents." However, the Organization for Cooperation and Security in Europe issued a report titled, "Human Rights Violations and Impunity in the Chechen Republic of the Russian Federation," which stated of the investigation that "the findings indeed do confirm the major allegations and show that there is a problem of total impunity of the security forces." The OCSE report recommends, among other measures, that world governments employ emergency measures to accept refugees from the region, as well as support nongovernmental organizations working to help queer Chechens escape persecution.[4]

These asylum seekers from Chechnya are most often relocated to South Africa, Belgium, Argentina, the Netherlands, and Sweden. As Marsha Gessen stated in her article, "The Year Russian L.G.B.T. Persecution Defied Belief":

> *For now, L.G.B.T. asylum seekers are still faring well in the U.S., but the application process takes years, and with the Trump Administration reshaping this country's immigration landscape, it's hard to imagine this country welcoming many Muslim gay men, even when they are fleeing mortal danger.*

While the fate of a gay man in Chechnya is uncertain, they are at least free to leave the region on their own. Lesbians in Chechnya face a more terrifying fate. Their lives are controlled entirely by their fathers, brothers, and husbands. Women are generally killed if thought to be gay.

So where are we today? In speaking with several people in the gay, lesbian, and transgender community in my sheltered corner of America, I learned that their fears are not of a diabolical Nazi-style concentration camp or modern-day Chechnya, but they still have very real concerns regarding discrimination, equal rights, health, safety, and quality of life.

Modern-Day Threats

THE REALITY OF HATE CRIMES create an environment of fear for the LGBTQ+ community. Like mass shooting incidents in schools that now happen with increasing regularity, hate crimes against LGBTQ+ individuals can come out of nowhere and they can be killed at random. According to a November 2017 FBI report, gay-hate crimes are on the rise, especially against transgender Americans. According to the FBI, of the single-bias hate crime incidents noted in 2016, 17.7 percent were motivated by sexual orientation, with a 43 percent increase in anti-transgender crimes from 2015 to 2016.[5] And a report from the National Coalition of Anti-Violence Programs (NCAVP) noted that homicides resulting from anti-LGBTQ hate crimes saw an 86 percent spike from 2016 to 2017.[6]

The transgender community faces significant daily issues with public restrooms. "My biggest fear right now is the bathroom; which one should I use? I don't feel safe in either one," said Drew, an asexual, non-binary person (who prefers the pronouns "they," "their," and "them") who agreed to speak with me at a local coffee shop. Drew explained that in the few years since coming out and beginning to transition from female to male, they have been blocked from using the ladies' bathroom because people perceive them as male. Drew is "terrified" of the men's bathroom, where they feel vulnerable. "I would prefer a single-door bathroom, a family bathroom, where I don't have to identify, and I don't have to fear," Drew said, adding, "And then there are the teens who have to deal with not only the bathrooms but the gym classes and showers," referring to teens' particular vulnerability.

Shannon, a transgender woman who transitioned while working at a large company after being employed there seventeen years, told of a transgender coworker who had faced discrimination regarding which bathroom she was allowed to use. Shannon's workplace initially instructed her coworker to use a single-stall bathroom in a specific area of the complex, about a half-mile round trip from where she worked. Shannon's coworker would often risk the backlash of the human resources department and use the women's restroom located in her immediate work area.

There were anti-discrimination policies in place by the time Shannon transitioned, but she was still on the receiving end of discrimination and retaliation. Other people using the restroom had taken to "tattling" on Shannon to human resources personnel, saying they felt it inappropriate that she used the women's restroom. Shannon stated it was never the women who were bothered by her bathroom use: "It was always, always, always men." Because Shannon was afraid to use the bathroom, her supervisor gave her a list of women's names in her department who were willing to escort her, to help her feel safe from harassment or worse on the way to the bathroom.

Shannon told me when people found out where she sat at work, they would come by just to "see the freak." Someone from HR ultimately started shadowing Shannon at least once per week in order to curtail any disparaging comments or remarks slung in her direction. Fortunately, one of Shannon's friends in HR had a transgender child and understood what she was going through. Shannon was grateful to have an ally at work, as this individual understood better than most how hurtful people's comments could be.

I am aware of an incident that occurred at a local music festival—a place most of us would consider to be generally accepting and where everyone is in good spirits. A transgender woman needed to use the restroom, but the person in charge at that venue ran the transgender woman out of the ladies' bathroom. The transgender woman then walked into the men's room and was subsequently run out by the same individual. Where, then, should this transgender woman go to answer the call of nature?

Transgender people are not the only ones concerned about their use of public restrooms. I heard from several gay men that they were also uncomfortable using public, multi-stall bathrooms, as they felt vulnerable at times and fearful of violence or slurs. Most would be more comfortable with a single-door (unisex) bathroom.

As of June 2018, only eighteen states and the District of Columbia have legislation that prohibits discrimination against transgender individuals in public conveniences.[7] Currently, an OSHA (Occupational Safety and Health Administration) guideline regarding restroom access for transgender workers states that all employees, including transgender employees, *should* (notice the word is should not must) have access to restrooms that correspond to their gender identity. This guide states that any bathroom restrictions could result in employees avoiding using restrooms entirely while at work, which could lead to potentially serious physical injury or illness. No specific laws on a federal level are in place to enforce these rights across the board.

Discrimination in Other Countries

CHRIS D., A MAN IN his mid-twenties, is a sign language interpreter in an elementary school. He is fearful of traveling abroad to certain countries. He said, "I would love to travel but there are places I could never go. Russia. I can never go to Russia." He then discussed the horrors for gay men in many countries, especially Muslim countries.

"My husband and I wanted to go to Belize, but at the time, foreigners who identified or who were perceived as homosexuals entering the country could face life in prison," he said. And then with a slight drop of his head, he explained that while his husband, Andy, does not immediately come across as gay, he does not have the "luxury" to pass as straight. Chris' voice is in a higher range than most men, his features more soft, and his demeanor and dress more effeminate. Chris believes these characteristics would "out" him as gay, therefore putting him at risk in certain foreign countries.

My son Hunter was nineteen when he decided to leave the States and move with his boyfriend to Australia. As his mother, I was terrified at the thought of him flying outside the country, worried about his gay demeanor and his outwardly gay appearance. While he was not flamboyant as such, he was certainly not a rough and tough athletic young man, nor a weathered-looking cowboy type—either of which may have been easier for him to pass as being straight. Hunter is slight of build with effeminate features and an alto pitch to his voice (the highest tone for a male), which is often mistaken as a female voice on the phone.

I feared him going to Australia, as I had learned of the dozens of gay men who were killed or had disappeared around Sydney some years before. Regardless of the time that had lapsed since the last of those reported hate crimes, I was afraid for his safety.

CHAPTER 3
It's Not a Choice

I AM SURE MOST OF us have at one time or another wondered if being gay or feeling trapped in the wrong gender was a choice. Many people contend that "homosexuality" and gender dysphoria are mental disorders and a person "suffering" these conditions can be cured if they so choose.

From my own experience, I knew my son was different before he did—I could see it and I could sense it. It took him years to reconcile for himself why he didn't fit in to the accepted behaviors as his brothers and his peers did. It wasn't about choice; it was about coming to an understanding and acceptance for himself. Lengthy studies have tried to discover a biological predisposition for a person to be gay or if a person's sexual and gender identity is a choice. Several studies have involved the Xq28 gene on the X chromosome—the so-called "gay gene." Thus far those studies have been inconclusive; however, some studies suggest sexual orientation tends to run in families and, therefore, it is likely to be somewhat genetic. I found this genetic suggestion interesting because in my son's case, his half-brother from his father is also gay. Unfortunately, by this admission, I can see where some people may point a finger at this, stating *blame* or *reason* for the two young men's orientation.

A common misconception is that only humans are attracted to the same sex, which fuels the assumption that male-female pairings are the only "natural" way. But there are many species in the animal kingdom that dispel this myth. Lions, chimpanzees, bison, dolphins, penguins, and over a hundred bird species have been observed engaging in homosexual activities. As these pairings do not result in offspring, there are many questions as to why animals participate in same-sex relationships. One theory is that this behavior forms strong social bonds within the animal's community. Others posit that it is just for fun. "Not every sexual act has a reproductive function," said Janet Mann, a biologist at Georgetown University.[8]

Sexual Attraction Is Natural

THERE IS NO CHOICE REGARDING sexual attraction for anyone. Nearly all the gay men and women I spoke with indicated they *tried to be straight* at some point before coming out. Ultimately, though, it was simply not natural for them, and they could not fake the rest of their lives living as straight people.

Interestingly enough, most of these individuals said they were "grossed out" by seeing straight public displays of affection. This isn't something that ever occurred to me. As uncomfortable as it is for most straight people to see gay people engage in a kiss or hold hands, most gay people feel the same watching their straight counterparts display affection.

Mark was a straight-looking boy born into a family of seven children in a staunchly Catholic household. He was a military kid, moving frequently, and was all-boy as he was growing up, enjoying anything masculine: sports, cars, hunting, fishing, chasing after girls, and having sex with girls. He could and did pass as straight. Mark explained that he tried to be straight, doing everything he could to fit the perceived normal male role but, later in life, could no longer fight off the truth of his identity. After a year of counseling with a priest, Mark realized there was no changing what he had felt all his life. He was different than his straight male family members and friends. Mark was gay.

This "not a choice" sentiment seems to be universal with gay and transgender persons. It also seems that many, if not a majority, make at least an attempt at performing in a straight or cisgender role ("cisgender" meaning the biology of one's birth).

Like everyone else I spoke with, my son Hunter fell into this category. I watched him try to date girls in his class and sneak porn magazines into his room, presumably to either see what the attraction was or to see if he had an attraction; I don't know and I didn't ask. He was awkward and uncomfortable regarding anything more than just friendship with women, and he had dozens and dozens of female friends. As an extrovert with an effervescent personality, Hunter also had scads of guy friends. He nearly always dressed like a very fashion-forward boy, with a few exceptions of wearing mom's heels and makeup as a gag. But there was always a side to him that was effeminate and that society would see as "girlish." He would always be my kitchen helper, the Christmas tree decorator, and the arts and craft kid.

I would learn later that he was uncomfortable around other boys and their need to display testosterone. He didn't quite understand their desire for contact sports and rowdy parties and "all that back slapping and crotch grabbing." Hunter, I believe, felt intimidated by the most macho of the boys in school, and as an adult, has often stated that he feels intimidated by most middle-aged, straight white men—an unfortunate overgeneralization on his part, perhaps, but his honest feelings nonetheless. I am unsure if his intimidation relates to a fear of physical harm or a fear of repression, or both.

None of Hunter's differences really caught me off guard, and I refused to put any of my three boys into a specifically designed box, expecting them to look a certain way or act a certain way. But nearly everything Hunter did on the outside of our family's walls conflicted with the boy that was growing up on the inside, in the safety of his own home with his family.

Hunter tried to be straight. He tried to fit in. He struggled with depression and had extremely dark, scary days when I worried every minute that I would come home and find he had taken his own life. Hunter wanted to be like his brothers, he wanted to be straight, but he wasn't. It was, at times, excruciating to watch him struggle to identify as gay, understand it, and finally accept it.

Whether it is social, psychological, or biological, as the mother of a gay person, I can attest, it is anything but a *choice*.

Political attitudes about sexual orientation are connected to people's understanding of same-sex behavior. People who believe that being gay is immoral tend to believe that sexuality is a choice or is influenced by social factors. Those who support free expression of sexuality tend to believe biological factors influence sexual orientation.[9]

Gender Fluidity Is Natural

TWO SPIRITS IS A TERM given to those in Native American or Indigenous tribes whose gender identity is fluid or referred to as a "third" gender—not specifically male, not specifically female. In years past, those who identified as *two spirits* were well-respected among tribes, dressed in either men's or women's attire, and acted in the highly regarded capacities of healer, counselor, or storyteller. The definition and names for these individuals vary by tribe and do not translate directly to lesbian, gay, or transgender.

These gender-fluid individuals threatened the European colonizers' heteronormativity in the mid-to-late 1800s. Therefore, the federal government removed thousands of *two spirits* from their tribes and their native lands, relocating them to the first federally funded off-reservation boarding school known as the Carlisle Industrial Indian School in Carlisle, Pennsylvania.

Today, depending on the religious beliefs of a tribal community, *two spirits* individuals may still be highly regarded or may be shunned, much like other transgender, marginalized people. *Two spirits* often become involved with local LGBTQ+ communities in order to find a place where they are accepted. However, *two spirits* are recognized as different from those in the traditional sense of the LGBTQ+ community, as *two spirits* want to reclaim their traditional indigenous ways and acceptance, while the LGBTQ+ community models their desire for acceptance after the civil rights movement.

Regardless of the differences or similarities in these people, those who identify as gay, transgender, or *two spirits* adamantly profess their identity is not a choice, and science appears to be more in agreement with that position.

Gender Confirmation Surgery (GCS): Who Would Choose This Path?

WHEN TALKING WITH PEOPLE IN the LGBTQ+ community, there was a resounding voice that I heard from all: "Why would I choose something so difficult?"

Before I began this project, I wondered what it was like to have a sex change (not that I wanted one; I just wondered how all the pieces and parts were created and put into place). When I learned what it entails to make sexual reassignment a reality, I quickly realized that changing one's gender was not something anyone would undergo on a whim.

It was suggested that I remove this section about GCS because it is too graphic and that it may get this book censored and possibly banned from sales in certain venues. I take exception to this, as the entire purpose of this writing is to educate people about the lives of those that many of us do not understand.

This section may be disturbing to the sensibilities of some. Please know that I researched these surgeries and use clinical terminology. I also ran this part past individuals who have been through these procedures to ensure they were not sensationalized. From those who have had these surgeries, I heard the following: "I would much rather people understood how much pain I endured with recovery from surgery, how I had to stare at a single feature in the texture of my ceiling while dilating to keep from screaming in pain. I would much rather they know that than 'commend' me on my 'bravery' for coming out."

I also heard, "I am not real satisfied with my surgery, as I wish it were done more cosmetically, but I am much happier with identifying this way than I was before the surgery. And yes, the recovery was difficult and it was painful."

One person said, "Please do not take this section out just to placate those who don't want to know about it—this is our real story and it is not always pretty."

Therefore, for those who have gone through this and have endured so much, I am choosing to keep this section intact. Please read about these surgeries at your own discretion.

Male to Female (MTF)

For a transgender female (a person born with male sexual assignment who identifies as female) several processes must take place prior to the reassignment surgeries from male to female (MTF). First, they are placed on female hormones, which inhibit testosterone, enhance breast growth, and essentially enable the feminine, softer features to come into play. They can then undergo breast augmentation if they either don't like the size of their hormone-induced breasts or don't want to wait for them to come on, like a young girl going through puberty. This breast enhancement surgery is referred to as "top surgery."

If a transgender female wants to complete the transition, she will undergo "bottom surgery." There are several options for this surgery. Vaginoplasty is the creation of a vagina. This can be done by using the patient's penile and scrotal tissue to create a vagina, clitoris, and labia. Some procedures utilize part of the colon to create part of the vagina. Another approach is to completely remove the male genitalia and create the vagina. In all cases, the testicles are removed, the urethra is shortened and placed into a female position, and the nerves in the penis head are preserved to form the clitoris. The cavity to the body is opened in order that penetration can be achieved.

For the first several months after surgery, the body's new cavity must be prevented from closing back up. The process is referred to as dilation. This involves the use of rods, which are of different lengths and widths, inserted to a prescribed depth and moved around within the cavity. Initially, the process takes approximately two hours per dilation cycle, and it is performed three times a day. The frequency is then cut to twice per day, and ultimately to about once per week for forty-five minutes. This was described to me in layman's terms as the same concept as a pierced ear; if you don't keep an earring in the hole, the body will naturally close it up. The process of dilation does not end and must be continued throughout the transgender woman's life.

Why would anyone choose to go through this if not for a total conviction of one's true identity?

Female to Male (FTM)

Someone who transitions from female to male (FTM) has similar issues to contend with. The individual must begin by taking testosterone to grow facial hair, deepen the voice, spread the shoulders, and generally bring on a more masculine appearance. He then has the option of top and bottom surgeries.

The top surgery involves the patient having his female breasts surgically removed. This process removes the breast tissue while preserving the nipple for grafting back onto a more male sculpted chest. The recovery requires cauliflower-like sponges called bolster dressings that are used to compress the nipple graft onto the chest wall to improve the chance that the grafted nipples will take.

In most cases, a patient will also require several days or weeks with a drain tube and bag in order to drain fluid collection at the site of the surgery. Without the proper drainage, seromas (fluid collections) can form which may require surgical intervention.

One option for bottom surgery for a transition is a vaginectomy, which is the equivalent of a hysterectomy followed by the surgical closure of the vagina. A metoidioplasty requires hormones to enlarge the female clitoris, which is then used, along with the labia, to relocate to a more forward position like a penis. A scrotoplasty or the creation of a scrotum can be accomplished with the dissection and rotation of the labia and insertion of silicone or saline testicle implants.

Phalloplasty is surgery that constructs a penis from a graft tissue usually taken from the forearm, back, leg, abdomen, or hip/groin. This surgery will allow the transgender male to experience erotic and tactile sensation, rigidity for sexual intercourse, and the ability to stand to urinate. This procedure requires a penile implant surgery, which is a device that helps inflate a flaccid penis. Phalloplasty surgery often includes a vaginectomy (removal of the vagina, including hysterectomy), urethroplasty, scrotoplasty, glansplasty (a procedure that constructs the bulbous structure at the top of the penis) and penile implant.

The recovery from these procedures is lengthy, painful, and likely underappreciated by those of us on the outside. Again, I say, who would do this type of grueling procedure if it were merely a choice?

The cost for these types of procedures is hefty. According to the Philadelphia Center for Transgender Surgery, a MTF bottom surgery starts at $19,500 and a FTM bottom surgery starts at $21,250. These are the beginning prices and are not inclusive of the top surgery, body surgery, and facial surgeries, which are all designed to enhance the preferred gender and inhibit one's previous gender.

These surgeries are cost prohibitive for most people, and only some insurances pay for certain procedures in specific cases. In other words, a transgender individual who desires to have their gender reassigned is either at the mercy of what insurance deems necessary, appropriate, or worthy—or they have a large personal bankroll to finance their reassignment.

Why People Take This Path

I MUST EMPHASIZE THIS AGAIN so that the point comes across: transitioning is extremely difficult, painful, expensive, and potentially risky to undergo, and so it is never done on a whim. Again, *Why would anyone simply choose to go through this if it were simply a choice and not a need?*

What is the *need?* The need is to cure the depression, the feeling of being a freak or knowing they are different, never fitting in, being told they are inhuman for their *choice* or that they will be damned to hell, having no protection from discrimination regarding their housing, their workplace or their *civil rights* (meaning the laws and customs that protect an individual's freedom in a given country or political system, such as life, safety, political and legal rights and protection from discrimination), and basic *human rights* (meaning the ways of living and being treated that everyone on the planet deserves by virtue of being human and do not vary by country or government, such as access to clean water, protection from torture and the right to fair trial). The *need* for the change is to stop the desire to want to die from years of faking their lives in a cisgender world. The *need* is to be perceived in the gender they identify with so as to stop the harassment, the slurs and the violence toward them.

Drew, whom we met earlier, who identifies as an asexual, non-binary person (preferring the pronouns "they," "them" and "their"), chooses to have an outward appearance of a male because they are more comfortable and identify more closely with the male gender than female gender.

Drew had top surgery recently and explained that they have no desire for bottom surgery because they have never had an intimate relationship in all of their fifty-plus years and feels no sexual attraction to either male nor female persons. They wanted their body to project that of a more neutral gender. Drew had spent several, quite uncomfortable years breast-binding in order to feel more comfortable with an image more closely matching their identity.

I would never have guessed Drew was not male. With the aid of testosterone, Drew has facial hair, a deeper voice and more masculine features overall; now without breasts, Drew cannot easily be identified as female by others. Yet, Drew tells me they still personally and socially struggle with their identity, even after hormones and top surgery. Perhaps some of Drew's struggle is a consequence of staying in the same place where they lived before their hormones and surgery. Drew still attends the same church and has the same circle of friends who knew Drew as female. Drew explained that many other people relocate in order to get a fresh start with their new identity.

Before transitioning, Shannon was a successful male with a wife, child, and professional career. She explained that she recognized after the suicide of a close family member that she too was going to end up dead if she didn't acknowledge her true need to be female. She said: "If I would have had a choice, I guarantee I would have taken the easy road. This is not the easy road." Shannon admits that, prior to her gender confirmation surgery, she was a closeted cross-dresser as a way to feel more comfortable with herself. She states that her wife was accepting with this behavior to a degree, so Shannon would openly wear women's clothing in her own home. However, when Shannon confided in her wife that she *needed* to move forward with transition, her wife could not, in all honesty to herself, remain married if it was to be to a woman.

Shannon ultimately went forward with her transition. She lost her wife of nearly seventeen years but kept her profession and her relationship with her son—and saved her own life. She is, as she puts it, "finally happy" and comfortable in her own skin. She is also in a budding new relationship with a female. Shannon is still attracted to females, so because of her now-female gender identity, she is considered lesbian.

Both Shannon and Drew wear a tattoo of a semicolon, as does Chris D., as a reminder of their own choice of life. Project Semicolon was created in 2013, using the punctuation mark—which signifies the continuation of a sentence, not its end—as a symbol of hope for those who may struggle with depression and suicidal ideation, or have survived a suicide attempt. The semicolon is worn by many, and it is often a way of expressing the depth of a person's struggle within themselves or between their identity and society.

Denial Doesn't Work

To "come out" for lesbian, gay, bisexual, or transgender people is to live an honest life without feeling they have to hide behind a false identity or pretend to be attracted to something they are not. Just like anyone else, some people in the LGBTQ+ community want to display their affection publicly and some do not. However, they all want to be free to express who they are and be allowed to acknowledge who is important to them. Denying these feelings and behaviors doesn't work and for many; continued denial makes life seem not worth living.

If you are missing something important in life—be it food, shelter, money, love, etc.—that absence is what we focus on most. This has been dubbed "scarcity mindset" and can affect many aspects of our lives. In the short term, most people can handle any form of scarcity, but over time, the scarcity becomes all-consuming, can become debilitating, and can actually manifest other problems, including health issues and psychosocial issues.

For those in the LGBTQ+ community, if they are not identifying honestly with their sexuality or their gender, they are missing a key component to their personal wellbeing; they are suffering with a type of *scarcity*, and therefore every other aspect of their lives is affected by that scarcity.[10]

By coming out and living their authentic life, those in the LGBTQ+ community can begin focusing on other areas of their lives and stop living with a scarcity mindset. They are able to be more efficient employees because they are not working with the fear of reprisal if their orientation or identity is discovered; they maintain healthier relationships because they are no longer living a lie with a partner or trying to be someone they are not to their family; and they can live healthier lives because they are less stressed, less fatigued, and less overwhelmed. Imagine living every day in fear for your safety, worried about losing your job or being anxious that your landlord will kick you out if your sexual orientation or gender identity is found out … you would quickly understand the scarcity mindset.

CHAPTER 4

The Dangers of Family Rejection

THE FEAR OF REJECTION AND losing the love of family or the community of church, and the fear of being singled out as different can be terrifying to LGBTQ+ youth. To be associated with a community that political or religious leaders express hatred or disdain for and label as "freaks" creates immense turmoil and upheaval in the lives of young people who are exploring their identity. This, along with the fear of being publicly ridiculed, attacked, or even killed because of who they are can be paralyzing.

Everything about the life of people in the LGBTQ+ community is affected by their identity. For example, they cannot always get products and services from just any service provider—they often have to find providers that are accepting of them and will deal with them fairly, honestly, and with respect. In many places, there are no laws in place to protect them from discrimination and inequality regarding service provision. For many, hostility and discrimination are the responses they come to expect as normal in their world. This not only includes a hostile work environment but also a hostile *life* environment. They can be refused housing and employment and be denied air travel and the right to vote if their perceived gender does not match their ID. The degree of severity varies with the local environment and culture in which they live.

I understand why some people find it difficult and awkward to have a child who is in the LGBTQ+ community, but it certainly wasn't a threat to me or my way of life when my son came out, so I did not push my son away because he was different than me. If you have feelings of anger, denial, or rejection toward your LGBTQ+ child or another's child, seek help from a professional or those around you (friends, family, church) to help you come to terms with this new reality. Review the resources I have included at the end of this book, and find a way to a new perspective for your sake, for the child's, and for those around you. When my son finally came out to me, I was equally relieved and uncomfortable. I had always known, at least suspected, he was gay and was waiting for him to recognize it and come out to me; it was not for me to decide his sexual orientation. But when he actually said the words to me, "Mom, I'm gay," the elephant in the room that had been living with the family for years turned into an entire herd of three-ton, long trunked animals squeezed into our tiny house. But we worked through it. We talked. We cried. We talked some more. I read. I reached out to others. We expressed our discomfort and had raw, honest conversations … and I never stopped loving him.

Having a transgender child come out is something I haven't experienced. However, I have spoken with transgender individuals and know of some parents with transgender children—and they experienced similar yet different emotions when that conversation happened.

In regard to a transgender child coming out (let's face it, we are all someone's child, regardless of our age), some of the factors are unique to each individual. For instance, a transgender person changes their gender identity and with that change comes the new name. Let's imagine Levi's situation. His parents have to adjust to the "death" of Andrea, the woman he was. Levi is not born; Levi just appears in Andrea's body. It's all very sudden for the family, but Levi wants everyone to understand what he has had years to sort through and come to terms with.

In all fairness, the Levis of the world need to give some grace to the rest of the world regarding their transition. And parents, while I can only imagine how difficult it is to lose Andrea and accept Levi, may I suggest that you do your best to remember this is your child and that the alternative to not accepting him is the potential loss of him … forever.

There are other unique issues a family must face when "Andrea" transitions. For example, what do you do with the photos of Andrea? How do you explain this to your friends? Who is Levi going to bring home as a partner and how will you relate to that person? Does this mean Levi is gay? Will he want gender confirmation surgery? So many questions! To answer your questions, find a counselor, find a support group (even in my small community there is one), go online and scour social media—I guarantee you are not alone with your fear, your concern, your worry, and the shame you hold secretly inside. Let go of it: you did nothing wrong, nor did Levi, nor Andrea for that matter. But do not give up on Levi. He is a person, he is still your child, and he will always need his family.

While my oldest son only transitioned in regard to his name and persona, not his gender or sexual orientation, it was still very difficult for our family to adjust. But we tried. We slipped up, we corrected ourselves, and we tried again. And the reward to all that trying was hearing my son say, "Momma, you never gave up on me." In regard to the name change of transgender people, in some cases they are okay with references to their dead name, but others find it highly insulting to even bring it up.

Support the individual's choice in this matter. It is their life and their name. I noticed that in cases where there was familial acceptance and support, many transgender people did not mind discussing their former life, identity, or name. Without support, however, there was a vehement disdain toward the former identity.

For the remainder of this chapter, I want to present some alarming statistics to support my plea to all parents to be loving to their LGBTQ+ children and for others to understand the pressure this community is under. Figures are boring unless you are a statistician—however, they are necessary to convey a point. I chose to predominantly use statistics regarding LGBTQ+ youth, as these reflect the turmoil and confusion youth feel as they try to navigate their natural difference and its mismatch with societal norms and, more importantly, their family's expectations.

When you read the stats in this chapter, keep in mind these are not merely numbers. These are someone's children. Perhaps your child has become one of these numbers, as mine has.

Homelessness

ACCORDING TO 2012 SURVEY DATA from the Williams Institute at the UCLA School of Law, 1.6 million youth experience homelessness each year in the United States, and 40 percent of those identify as LGBT. LGBT youth represent about 7 percent of the population, which puts the 40 percent figure in sharper perspective.[11]

Some 46 percent of homeless LGBT youths run away because of family rejection of their sexual orientation or gender identity, 43 percent were forced out by parents, and 32 percent faced physical, emotional, or sexual abuse at home.

The National Alliance to End Homelessness reports that compared to all youth, young LGBTQ people have experienced double the rates of sexual abuse before age twelve.

"I didn't know how to talk to my family about being gay, and I was afraid of what my parents would think, so I left home," Taylor, a young immigrant from New Zealand explained of his experience of coming out. "I was only gone a week," he said with a shrug, as if a week without a place to live was no big deal. In Taylor's case, he was not forced out of his family's home, nor was he abused. But due to his family's religious convictions and his fear of their lack of acceptance of him for being part of the LGBTQ+ community, he felt they would not understand and feared their response. He felt it would be easier if he just left home.

Taylor was fortunate. His family was understanding and accepted him for who he was—a gay male. He admits that his mum cried and was concerned about his safety, but overall his family was readily accepting. His situation could have turned out much differently, and it does for a significant number of LGBTQ+ youth.

Where do these young people go when they are forced out or leave their homes? Many go into foster care and short-term shelters, but often these young people end up on the street where they are victimized and abused at a disproportionately higher rate than their non-LGBTQ+ youth counterparts.

Shelters sound like a safe place to stay and regroup; however, physical and sexual abuses are perpetrated on this group of youth within homeless shelters in alarming numbers, especially the young transgender population. Often, shelters force these young people to stay in the dorms or houses based on their gender at birth, not their identified gender, leaving them confused and vulnerable.

Harassment, assault, and rape within these shelters are common experiences, and data shows that half of the sampling of lesbian and gay youth who have stayed at these shelters reported a preference of living on the streets rather than staying in the hostile environments they found in these settings.[12]

Homeless LGBTQ youth are at greater risk for experiencing high levels of hardship, including higher rates of assault, prostitution (exchanging sex for money, food, shelter, and clothing), and early death. Black LGBTQ youth, especially young men, have the highest rate of homelessness.[13]

All of these statistics are just numbers until you know some of these people. They are daughters and sons, sisters and brothers. They are people with dreams and hopes, individuals who just want to feel safe, have a place to live, and food to eat.

There is no right or wrong feelings regarding the coming out of a friend or family member, but there are some human *rights* and some deplorable *wrongs*. The "rights" are pretty easy, in my opinion: All persons deserve fair (equal) and respectful treatment. All persons deserve to feel safe without discrimination. And in an effort to be completely transparent about my feelings, I do not believe that one person or group of people should receive extra, additional, or special accommodations with the exception of people with disabilities. People should simply be treated equally and fairly, including those in the LGBTQ+ community.

The "wrongs" are pretty much all other horrible atrocities, such as denying another person the ability to find housing or employment on the basis of sexual orientation or gender identity, the existence of criminal statutes that persecute LGBTQ+, the weak prosecution of those committing harassment, as well as hate crimes targeting this marginalized community. It is also wrong, I believe, to tolerate people and businesses denying services to LGBTQ+ persons by claiming it would go against their religious beliefs. It is wrong to commit violence toward persons that are LGBTQ+. And, it is wrong to spew overt hate toward those who are different from what any institution or authority has arbitrarily decided is the social norm.

When I asked LGBTQ+ people what they thought could help stop someone becoming one of these statistics, every one of them said, "The family needs to be supportive."

"We need to realize we need to accept our children if they are gay. Love them and let them know we are there to support them and treat them right," said William Mathis, who believes that his gay daughter's suicide was in part due to her feelings of being unaccepted.

"Parents need to support their kids," Chris D. said. "Hurt and abandonment is a big part of our community."

This community feels abandoned and betrayed by the ones who told them, when they were growing up, "I will never stop loving you." What they hear in retrospect is, "I will never stop loving you as long as you are straight and cisgender, otherwise you are no longer my child and I will love you less."

Suicide

DREW SAID, "THE ATTEMPTED SUICIDE rate is 41 percent among transgender people, and in the general public, it is around 1 percent." I verified these numbers were correct. What Drew didn't say, however, was the attempted suicide rate in the transgender population in the 18–44 age group was even higher—45 percent. Drew admitted to making several attempts to end their life, stating lack of acceptance and support as the main reasons. Family rejection is devastating to a young person's psyche. "Support your kid!" Drew told me.

Males in the United States represent 79 percent of all suicides, and gay men before the age of twenty-five are at an especially high risk of attempting suicide. A study of youth in grades seven through twelve found that lesbian, gay, and bisexual youth were more than twice as likely to have attempted suicide than their straight peers. Risk factors include hostile environments.[14]

Unfortunately, there is not much data available regarding the transgender population. One figure states 40 percent of transgender adults reported having made a suicide attempt. Of these, 92 percent reported having attempted suicide before the age of twenty-five.[15]

The most profound statistic is that *each episode* of victimization of someone who is LGBTQ, such as physical or verbal harassment or abuse, increases the likelihood of self-harming behavior by 2.5 times, on average.[16] *That was EACH EPISODE*, meaning even an offhand gay slur. Every discriminatory comment on television directed to the transgender community, every religious leader heard saying those in the LGBTQ community are going to hell, *every* incident, no matter how big or small, increases their likelihood of self-harm behavior by 2.5 times.

After a lifetime of negativity surrounding their sexual orientation or gender identity, people are tired, worn out, and frail in their soul. Research shows that gay or bisexual adults have higher rates of mood and anxiety disorders than straight people, and depression in LGB adults is usually rooted in discrimination and victimization from childhood and adolescence.[17] (Research on transgender people is lacking.)

I saw the torment in my child's eyes when he was figuring out his sexual orientation. I watched his days turn black. I watched his usual sunny disposition turn to one of doom and gloom. I know what it feels like to wonder if you will come home to find your child had too much to cope with and decided to take their life. I was fortunate; my child never attempted suicide—but not because he didn't think about it. He told me that when he was older. He said he was confused and felt alone regarding his sexual orientation as a younger man. And as loving, open, and understanding as I would like to believe I am, my child still had doubts and reservations about my level of commitment to loving and supporting him. We were not a perfect family, but I think we were a fairly good one, yet even that wasn't enough to ease my son's anguish. The point here is that even under good circumstances, people in the LGBTQ+ community are at an extreme disadvantage as they grow and find their way in life. They need our love and our unending support.

I recently attended my first PFLAG support meeting (the acronym originally stood for Parents, Friends of Lesbian and Gay but has become inclusive of transgender persons, although the acronym has not changed). It was an eye-opening experience. And while I cannot discuss what was talked about with any specificity because what is said there stays there, I can speak to the way I *felt* about what I heard and saw. There were far more people in attendance than I had anticipated, thinking it would be maybe three or four, but it was triple that. The room was filled with people of all sexual orientations and gender identities, and nearly everyone there was in their twenties. I knew only one person, my friend Drew, an asexual, non-binary person who had invited me.

The mood of the room was initially lighthearted. Everyone apparently knew each other and their back stories, but the atmosphere shifted to a serious, somber tone once the moderator pulled out a patchwork stuffed animal she called Elliot. Elliot was apparently the equivalent of a talking stick and whoever held Elliot had the floor. As any new, polite guest would do, I mostly listened, sitting back in the too-soft couch that basically swallowed me up, and took in what was being said. I had no expectation as to what would happen at this meeting or what I would hear.

I discovered there was a common thread among these young gay, lesbian, and transgender people, and it was *desperation.* They were desperate to be heard, desperate to be understood, desperate not to be judged, and above all, desperate to be loved. I learned snippets of their lives and their struggles, mostly with their parents, regarding their transitioning or coming out. I heard how their living situations consisted of couch surfing, trying to find a space to stay for a short time where people would accept them. In the terminology of homelessness, these young people fall into Category 2, so-called by the Housing and Urban Development agency (HUD), which refers to a person imminently at risk of losing their housing. They are staying with friends, living in a hotel, somewhere where they cannot be forever—they are a week or two from being on the streets.

For the most part, these young people were quiet, polite, and very introverted, almost to the point of looking like a beaten animal. When they spoke, they would keep their heads down and their eyes lowered, averting their gaze from the others in the room, apparently on the verge of tears, according to the tremble I heard in most their voices. They were obviously alone, lonely, and likely scared. They spoke of their work and family struggles and issues within their personal relationships. But mostly what I heard were the questions, "Why can't I just find a nice boyfriend?" "Why can't my parents just understand?" "Why does my mother do that?" There was a lot of conversation about mothers, perhaps because these young people lived mostly with their moms, or perhaps it was the mother-child bond that these young people were needing and not receiving. As a mom myself, I was shocked and saddened that the evening seemed to center around the failings of moms.

An even more profound and disturbing part of the evening was the feeling of hopelessness and defeat in the room. These young people were simply trying to be their authentic selves, but they had already seen so much pushback and backlash that they had become withdrawn and timid. I could almost *see* suicide in the room, as if it were an apparition circling, pausing in front of whoever was holding Elliot, waiting to pounce.

There was nothing I could do to fix these hurting people, no words that could act as a salve to heal their wounds, but the mom in me could not sit there without saying something. I asked for Elliot and hoped I could find something meaningful to say to this hurting group. I looked each of them in the eye, told them how courageous they were and how proud I was to be in their company. I, this straight, cisgender person who felt almost invasive sitting in with them, gay son or not, did my best to let each of them know they mattered, not to give up on themselves, and not to give in to the pressures around them.

My tiny voice of one was likely forgotten by morning, but I prayed it mattered to them. I prayed these young, struggling individuals would not let that apparition into their lives and that they would continue to go on living without joining the Semicolon Project for people who have attempted suicide. I left that evening frightened for each one of those young people and desperately needing to run home and hug my own gay son.

We don't have to like what is happening, and we don't have to understand it. But we must continue to love and support our children and do our best to accept them for who they are and leave the judgment to a higher power.

Violence

VIOLENCE TOWARD YOUTH IN THE LGB community (again, lacking sufficient data in most areas on transgender persons) has some shocking numbers behind it. According to data from the 2015 national Youth Risk Behavior Survey (YRBS):

- 10 percent of LGB students were threatened or injured with a weapon on school property
- 34 percent were bullied on school property
- 28 percent were bullied electronically .
- 23 percent who had dated or went out with someone during the twelve months before the survey had experienced sexual dating violence in the prior year
- 18 percent had experienced physical dating violence
- 18 percent had been forced to have sexual intercourse at some point in their lives[18]

This survey also showed that transgender people were four times more likely than the general population to report living in extreme poverty, making less than $10,000 per year, which sometimes pushes them to enter the dangerous trade of sex work. And nearly 80 percent of transgender people reported experiencing harassment at school when they were young.

In 2014, sixteen of twenty LGBT people who were murdered were people of color, according to the NCAVP (National Coalition of Anti-Violence Programs)—eleven were transgender women, and ten were transgender women of color.[19]

It is difficult to find good data on violence committed on transgender persons, as police and social workers have no unified system to track whether a person is transgender. Often transgender people are lumped into the category of their birth assignment, not the gender they identify with, and therefore the numbers and statistics of crimes and murders perpetrated upon transgender people is knowingly and notably skewed.

The transgender people I have spoken with assured me anecdotally that a very high number of violent crimes are perpetrated against the transgender population that are misrepresented due to the victim's gender being noted as that assigned at birth. The NCAVP notes that Bureau of Justice Statistics estimate there could be as many as forty times more hate crimes occurring nationally than the FBI reports.

Violence, however, is not limited to physical assaults and verbal condemnation—it is also prominent in the form of sexual violence: rape, harassment, coercion. Here is just one story.

Nichole was a thriving teenager in a small school. She was struggling with her sexual identity and was coming out as lesbian when a female coach/administrator befriended her and became her mentor.

Nichole became sexually involved with this woman, causing among other things, lasting strife and turmoil to Nichole's developing self-esteem and character. Nichole's perpetrator would ultimately be convicted of several sexually related crimes against Nichole and another young girl and imprisoned for years.

Nichole has spent years trying to recover and regain her identity and strength following that abuse. She has struggled continually with anxiety, depression, self-harm, and suicidal ideation; on at least one occasion she attempted to take her own life. As a woman now in her mid-twenties, many years after her victimization, Nichole is attempting to move beyond her trauma. She is currently in a healthy, age-appropriate relationship with another young woman and doing her best to find her way.

Her family, rather than unifying and rallying around her, became divided over the fact that she is lesbian. During the years following her trauma, rather than accepting and loving Nichole as a total person and helping her heal and feel unconditionally loved, certain members of her family chose to partition their love of her: loving the person but rejecting her sexuality on Biblical grounds. This has devastated Nichole emotionally and hampered her ability to heal. She has had to navigate her sexuality and also rationalize that her family doesn't actually blame her for her sexual assault—all this at a time when she is also trying to figure out how to transition from being a teenager to an adult.

Nichole's family professes their love of her through social media and in person, affirming their love of her with hugs and kisses but then refusing to acknowledge her partner. Some won't allow their children to be around her, saying she is "unhealthy" for them and avoiding anything relating to her sexuality. At one point, Nichole was engaged to be married to a woman and one uncle told her he loved her but would not accept her marriage and would not attend her wedding. Nichole said, "This broke my frickin' heart." Nichole's mother encouraged her not to *invite the family to the wedding to avoid the harsh, hurtful rejections she would likely receive.*

Her scars run deep. She is deeply religious but feels unworthy because she has been told bad things about her sexuality by her family and religious leaders. She has had to compartmentalize the trauma of her sexual assault, separate from her sexual identity, and learn to cope with her family's strings-attached love.

She said, "I think I am healing pretty well from it [the sexual assault], *but the family thing … I don't think I will ever get over that."*

How can we stop these crimes against our children (remember, every person is someone's child)? We must become educated and stand up.

Community-based programs are places to meet and feel safe. Support groups for families are necessary to better understand what their child is going through. Parents and siblings can also find comfort with others going through the same transition in their family.

As for how to stop crimes of violence of any kind against LGBTQ+ youth, *if you see something, say something*: do not stand by and watch someone being harassed, bullied, or hurt. Do the right thing for everyone, not just the straight, cisgender population. This is our duty as human beings. LGBTQ+ people are just trying to find their way in this life, as we all are. What else can be done?

- **Teachers and administrators** need to become more educated on how to curb bullying and instill acceptance in their students. We need to create safe spaces where young LGBTQ+ students can go and seek help without fear of retribution, including discrimination and bullying by adults.
- **Counselors and social workers** need to ensure safety in shelters and make appropriate, individualized classifications and housing decisions based on gender identity, not birth assignment.

- **Welfare services** need to provide safe and supportive facilities and foster families for LGBTQ+ youth that have been forced to leave their homes or are running from dangerous situations.
- **The local community** can display LGBTQ+ supportive signs and symbols that indicate a safe space for those within that community. Facilities, businesses, and even homes can send a clear message of support and safety by displaying images such as pink and blue triangles (the symbol of transgender), rainbows, or safe-zone stickers. LGBTQ+ youth are quick to pick up on these cues from their environment.[20]
- **Police** need to learn how damaging it can be to force a young person back into a situation where they feel their sexual orientation or gender identity puts them at risk.
- **Courts** need to invoke their authority and hand down harsh punishment for hate crimes.
- **Legislators** need to pass anti-discrimination and inclusion laws that will protect all persons, including gay and transgender persons.
- **Parents** need to listen to their children, withhold judgmental feelings and remember this is *not a choice*. Stop gender shaming. They should encourage their children to be who they are without fear of retribution. Above all, parents need to support and love their children.

Illness

The foundation of success in life is good health: that is the substratum fortune; it is also the basis of happiness. A person cannot accumulate a fortune very well when he is sick.
—**P.T. Barnum**

WE ALL UNDERSTAND THE NEED for good physical and mental health. Many people have the ability to obtain healthcare, but many *do not*. Often the reasons for lack of healthcare are universal: lack of finances, lack of accessibility, and lack of education. However, the LGBTQ+ community has unique circumstances that add to their overall lack of access to good healthcare, such as difficulty finding providers that understand and accept the specific, unique health challenges faced by LGBTQ+ people, as well as finding a provider they feel safe and comfortable with.

Income is an obvious reason for suffering poor health and lack of healthcare. Low income is also prevalent in the LGBTQ+ community. A study by the Williams Institute in September 2018 suggests that sexual minorities in the United State have fewer economic resources than their straight peers. These hardships are more pronounced in the gay/bi/trans female population, who are more likely to be "near poor" and in receipt of public assistance than straight women. These women were also less likely to complete a college education and were twice as likely to be unemployed.

While sexual minority men were more likely to have earned a college degree than straight men, they earned less money and reported more economic hardship than their straight counterparts.

This indicates possible wage discrimination.[21]

It goes without saying that if a person is financially challenged, they are less likely to receive good—if any—healthcare. But healthcare starts at home as a young person and includes a healthy understanding of yourself and who you are. Children learn the bulk of who they are from the examples and behaviors of their parents. Successful children are generally encouraged by their parents to be anything and anyone they want to be. "You can grow up and be the president of the United States" and "You could be a doctor, lawyer, or astronaut if you want" are statements many parents tell their young children. But do parents consider this could include their child being gay or transgender? Are parents prepared to have open dialogue about this and support their gay, transgender, or curious child?

Some parents (I would presume more often parents who are gay or transgender) see the need to educate their children to explore and accept their sexual orientation and gender identity, but straight, cisgender parents may not consider this. I can honestly say it never crossed my mind to discuss gender identity with my children. Sensing that I had a gay son did lead me to parent differently than my peers, I believe, as I knew I needed to keep the sexual orientation of my child in the forefront of any conversation regarding health and sexuality. "You can be anything you want, son, and it is okay for you to love anyone," I would tell him and his brothers. Yet even with my affirmation, Hunter still struggled to believe he would be accepted.

In my conversations with those in the LGBTQ+ community, sexual orientation and gender identity were not subjects *never* addressed by parents or schools in sex education programs, regardless of whether it was known there were gay or transgender children present.

Shannon, a transgender woman, explained it well when she said that, while her parents never specifically said anything derogatory about her interest in stereotypical feminine toys or behaviors, she was dissuaded or redirected toward the standard male toys and behaviors. She stated, "No one had to tell me that what I felt inside wouldn't be accepted by society. There are many cues along the way and clues, like the second that you, as a [male] child, show an affinity toward girly things, someone will redirect you. It might be a soft redirect or it might not be, but enough of those times build and, you know, *Okay, I'm supposed to behave this way and the second I deviate from that path, people are going to treat me differently*."

Shannon, like most transgender people, has experienced how difficult it is when parents "gender" their children. She says:

> *We pink and blue them. Some people want to go to the complete extreme opposite and say it's best to raise your children in a genderless way. I don't know if that is the right answer either. In fact, the odds are your kid is going to be born with certain genitalia, and their gender is going to match that and will be consistent. There is no sense in ignoring that fact. In my case, if, when I was playing with dolls, my parents had given me just a little bit of leeway to figure that out, perhaps I would have had the confidence to tell someone.*

"I never got the sex talk," Chris D. said, speaking of his parents. "I wonder how many gay people have gotten the sex talk that is not just the assumption that you are straight. And what does the sex talk look like as a straight parent talking to your gay child?" he asked me. I was surprised by Chris' question but felt compelled to tell him. He is the same age as my sons, and I felt a maternal pull toward him for that reason, as well as for his wounded heart regarding his own family's avoidance of him. "I did and still do speak to my son about sex, about safe sex, and about relationship issues," I told Chris. "I tell him similar things that I tell his straight brothers: Use a condom, get checked for STDs—which he now tells me are referred to as STIs (sexually transmitted infections) to include HIV—and to know your HIV status."

I also told Chris I have always talked to all my sons about the proper way to treat their partners—to be respectful and considerate, kind and loving, and to expect the same in return. I feel these are the cornerstones to healthy relationships, whether they are straight or gay.

Chris, who often uses humor to cover his hurt, said of himself about his lack of sex education, "Why do I need a condom? I'm not going to get pregnant!" In a serious tone, he added, "I think there is a lack of education. Parents don't have the sex talk [with their children] or don't know how to have it."

He added:

> *I never got the sex talk in school either, through sex education. I think schools should discuss sex education and include education on "gay sex." Not everyone is straight. I also didn't get the support regarding a breakup. All teenagers going through a breakup think it's the end of the world. My parents would console my siblings, do the TV rom-com parent thing, but I didn't get that. If I had breakups, it was traumatic and I would cry; my parents would give me distance. Where they would go to my siblings' rooms and console them, I had to work it out myself.*

To Chris's point, the Guttmacher Institute released the following statistics regarding sex and HIV education as of February 1, 2019: Twenty-four states and the District of Columbia require sex education in schools; thirty-four states and the District of Columbia require education on HIV and AIDS; and thirteen states require that if provided, sex education must be "medically, factually, and technically accurate."

Of those states that teach sex education only eight of them are required to provide instruction that is "appropriate for a student's cultural background and not be biased against any race, sex, or ethnicity."

There are only twelve states that require discussion of sexual orientation. Nine of those require discussion of sexual orientation to be inclusive and three require "only negative information on sexual orientation."[22]

In 2017, it was estimated that 150,000 youth aged thirteen to seventeen identified as transgender in the United States, which equates to approximately 0.7 percent. And 0.6 percent of U.S. adults (1.4 million individuals) identified as transgender.[23] A 2016 study by the Center for Disease Control found that approximately 8 percent of high school students identified as gay, lesbian, or bisexual, which, at the time, was approximately 1.3 million youths. This shows that a significant number of youths are being uneducated about *their* sex in schools where only straight sex education is taught. (Note: These numbers are only the students who have identified as transgender or gay and does not include those who are curious, unclear, or simply too scared to come out.)

It should also be noted that those in the LGBTQ+ community have difficulty with the healthcare system in general, finding it hard to locate providers who are educated on their specific needs, as well as finding providers who are respectful of their patients' identities.

Based on the near, at, or below poverty levels of many in the LGBTQ+ community, healthcare is often seen as simply too expensive and gone without. It is my presumption that fear of being misunderstood or judged by providers may also keep many LGBTQ+ individuals away from healthcare providers. This is consistent with data from a Williams Institute generation study that found that only 4 percent of sexually active gay and bisexual men in the United States use PrEP (pre-exposure prophylaxis) to prevent the transmission of HIV. The study also found that most sexually active gay and bisexual men aged eighteen to twenty-five are not tested for HIV annually as recommended, and 25 percent of young men have never been tested.[24]

Rejection within the family leads to substantially higher numbers of illegal drug use, depression, suicide attempts, and high risk for HIV and STDs. According to the Williams Institute, compared with young LGBTQ people who were not rejected or felt they were only slightly rejected by their parents and caregivers, highly rejected young LGBTQ people had the following characteristics:

- More than eight times as likely to have attempted suicide;
- Nearly six times as likely to report high levels of depression;
- More than three times as likely to use illegal drugs; and
- More than three times as likely to be at high risk for HIV and STDs.[25]

To put these statistics into a more personal, relatable context, the following applies to the transgender and LGB individuals I have spoken with:

- *Every one* of them has made an attempt at self-harm and/or suicide;

- The *large majority* have had times of housing insecurity;
- *80 percent* were bullied in school;
- *Many* do not seek routine or maintenance healthcare due in large part to not feeling safe or comfortable;
- *None* had sexual orientation or gender identity sex education in school; and
- *Every one* of them has some sense of "difference" within their family based on their orientation or gender identity.

In other words, we have a long way to go in understanding the needs of LGBTQ+ in order that they feel confident, comfortable, healthy, and safe.

CHAPTER 5
Religion vs. Human Rights

"Worry about your own sins. You won't be asked about mine."
—Toby Mac

ANTINOUS (BORN A.D. 111) MAY be the first documented gay man, although during his lifetime, pederasty (sexual relations among men and boys) was common in Greek society and had been for centuries. Known for his beauty, Antinous became the lover of Hadrian, the ruler of the Roman world. After Antinous' death at the young age of nineteen, Hadrian elevated him to the status of a god. It has been stated that the effect of this religion may be what prompted Christians to turn against same sex relationships, a prejudice that, in large part, still exists to this day.

In modern society, there are three major stances in organized religion regarding same sex relationships: rejectionism, "love the sinner, hate the sin," and full acceptance.

Rejectionism

REJECTIONISM IS THE PRACTICE OF refusing or ignoring a certain policy. Fundamentalist denominations of the Judeo-Christian and Muslim religions object to gay relationships and the rights of gay people. Several countries punish being gay by sentencing those caught engaging in sexual practices to torture or death. Others of these rejectionist groups believe in "conversion therapy," i.e., prayer-based "cures" for being gay, transgender, or otherwise queer. And God can forgive the "sinners" if they give sincere efforts to repent and renounce their sexual orientation.[26]

Certain U.S. states have enacted legislation to make it illegal to use prayer-based conversion therapy on minors. Representative John McCrostie of Idaho's District 16 has attempted to get a bill passed in his state banning this type of practice, but he has been unsuccessful so far (at time of writing). As a gay man, Representative McCrostie is familiar with conversion therapy practices. "It's frightening, it absolutely is," he stated.

Conversion therapy is generally religiously motivated and is intended to change sexual orientation or gender identity to fit straight or cisgender normalities. Its practices include talk therapy, shock therapy, and aversion therapy. The "patients" are subjected to regular, intense, hours-long sessions where they are stripped of their identity and individuality and then built back up in the manner that represents what the practitioner desires them to be. In the case of the LGBTQ+ community, the hope is the subjects would no longer identify as gay or transgender, and begin to identify as straight and cisgender.

While there are no concrete statistics regarding the long-term effects of conversion therapy, there are studies that show over 40 percent of those forced to undergo conversion therapy practices attempt suicide.

In 2016, only five states had banned conversion therapy. By 2018, that number had risen to only eleven states, plus the District of Columbia.

"Love the Sinner, Hate the Sin"

"LOVE THE SINNER, HATE THE sin" holds that while LGBTQ people should be regarded with equal respect, their homosexual behavior should not be tolerated. This philosophy holds the perspective that while sexuality cannot be changed, a person should abstain from acting on their homosexual desires.[27]

Nichole, a young lesbian woman, told me through her tears of how certain members of her family once referred to her as one of the Godliest people in their family. This was before she came out. She states those same people have now told her in varying ways that she cannot be a child of God because she is gay; she cannot love God because she is gay; and she cannot go to church because she is gay.

Others who may not have actually heard these types of statements *feel* them with the hellfire and brimstone slung their way when church members learn they are LGBTQ+. While preaching the gospel that we should all love our neighbor, these church members also feel that LGBTQ+ people aren't worthy of the church or the love of God because of their sexual orientation or gender identity.

Full Acceptance

FULL ACCEPTANCE IS JUST THAT—THE person and their sexual orientation are accepted as with their straight counterparts. Under full acceptance, a church takes an egalitarian stance (belief that all people are equal and deserve equal rights and opportunities) and believes all people are accepted by God, regardless of sexual orientation and gender identity.[28]

Churches have been formed specifically for the purpose of being all-inclusive, as they have recognized this as an issue in traditional religious settings. Carolyn, an advocate ally to those in the LGBTQ+ community, explained that the Presbyterian denomination, the church she belongs to, only recently changed (2011) its bylaws to allow full inclusion of all persons, including gay and transgender persons. Her specific Presbyterian church was always inclusive and supportive of the LGBTQ+ community, and (as of 2015) it can perform same-sex marriages because of the change in bylaws. It apparently takes a change in bylaws for a church denomination to recognize their judgment issues and decide to make inclusion part of their culture.

"When you identify yourself as a Christian and say you love all people and then proceed to spew judgment and false claims, and use the Bible as a weapon, and to speak of your persecution, you are not being a follower of Christ in that moment," Carolyn said as her personal testimony at a city council hearing about passing an anti-discrimination ordinance.

Carolyn explained to the council, "I have had so many kids share with me the fear and hurt they've experienced because they are lesbian, gay, bisexual, or transgender. These kids have been rejected by their families, their churches, their friends, their youth leaders, and more, simply because of the way they were born."

She went on to say, "They [LGBTQ+ persons] are bullied and picked on and feel unsafe in their schools and community. Our youth are hurting and they are afraid. As a person of faith, I am not okay with that."

Members of Carolyn's church attend their local Pride celebration each year and offer a space for those in the LGBTQ+ community to receive a hug and an apology for any mistreatment they have experienced in the name of religion. They also encourage people to write down their stories of hurt inflicted upon them by the church. The church then shares these stories with the congregation, encouraging them to pray for the "least of these."

Mark, a former priest who came out as gay nine years into his time at seminary, talked with me at length regarding his Catholic upbringing and current beliefs. "I will always be Catholic," he said, "but I don't practice Catholicism any longer. I do still believe in God, but I also believe in a Supreme Being." He chuckled and added, "with lots of children who are chosen to teach us what we need to learn."

Mark struggled with his sexual identity for years, doing anything that appeared straight to push it aside—dating girls in high school, experimenting with sex with women, and then becoming a priest. "I put my sexuality in a box so I didn't have to deal with it. I figured if I was a priest, I wouldn't have to address it," he said.

Research shows there is no correlation between pedophilia and gay sexual orientation; however, this seems to be a misconception for many people. Unfortunately, with the current climate of publicized sexual abuse uncovered in the Catholic Church and the recent convictions of many priests for pedophilia, the research has been undermined from the public's perspective.

I asked Mark the difficult question about whether he was ever worried that people might question him on this matter after leaving the seminary. He replied, "Yes, I very much worried that people might accuse me of pedophilia if they knew I was homosexual. Thank God, no one ever did."

Mark attended more than a year's worth of counseling prior to coming out to his family and friends; he feared what their opinion of him would be, a man of the cloth, a brother to six siblings, and the son of fundamentalist religious parents. Mark was fortunate to be accepted by his family. He stated, however, that the anguish and turmoil he suffered in trying to cope with his fear of coming out was worse than the brain cancer he now endures.

Chris T. grew up with a fundamentalist Baptist background and attended a Christian university. He knew from the time he was a little kid that he was gay, but still he researched religion for years, trying to make sense of the two and how they could fit together. Chris's viewpoint is that John R. Rice, who Chris termed as the "father of fundamentalism," had a hand in encouraging the Bible Belt to present a united front against gay sexual orientation as a whole.

True or perceived, pressure from any group on an entire community of people can obviously cause rifts and separation, especially if those groups are religious in nature. We all want to be accepted, but it is hard for LGBTQ+ people to believe in a higher power that's greater than themselves when judgment from religious groups is so hurtful. Chris T., like Mark, now believes in a higher power, but not in God, per se. Chris is jaded, hurt, and bitter toward "standard" religious beliefs.

Chris D., on the other hand, found an open church that loved him unconditionally. Chris is an out gay man whose family never embraced his orientation. He states his family was never openly opposed to his sexuality, but they avoided the topic and anything pertaining to it, leaving Chris bewildered and often confused as a teen. While in high school, Chris came to find his current church, which he and his husband now call their "church home."

Taylor, a young gay man, grew up in a traditional Christian family where he, his siblings, and parents attended weekly service as parishioners and performed in the church's worship band. Taylor explained that he did not experience harassment from the church, but his mother did. According to Taylor, "Mum is still quite religious; she just no longer goes to church."

"So, your mom essentially picked you over the church and the congregation?" I asked Taylor.

"Yah, I guess so," he said with a chuckle and a bit of pride. I learned later from Taylor's mother that his recollection was not exactly on point regarding her decision to stop attending church, but she did find herself defending her son and choosing her love for him over the parishioners who spoke negatively about him and his sexual orientation.

Drew has seen great change in the church they have attended on and off since the 1980s. "Back in the day, there were no same-sex marriages, no openly gay or trans parishioners, just a lot of people who were still hiding while loving God," Drew said. Happily, that church established change and is now affirmative and openly diverse, accepting all people without discrimination. Drew states with satisfied laugher, "Now there are some days at my church where a heterosexual person may be a minority."

Drew, who seems very strong of faith, gave me a business card that they leave with people they feel could benefit by it that reads:

> *FYI, you have just shared space with a transgender person.*
> *The world did not come to an end, nobody tried to "turn you*
> *trans," and no children were harmed in any way. Transgender*
> *people are children of God, like you are, and we are simply*
> *trying to be who we are created to be.*

A video appeared on social media recently featuring an older gentleman, Mr. William Mathis, who was a guest on the *Ellen DeGeneres Show*. He lost his gay daughter to suicide when she had not felt accepted regarding her sexual orientation. Mr. Mathis said to Ellen, "Due to the way she was treated by her father and others, she took her own life."

I had the privilege to speak with Mr. Mathis, now a retired peanut farmer in Alabama. He explained to me that he was taught throughout his life that gay people were essentially rejects, even if they had been baptized and had accepted Christ as their savior. Mr. Mathis felt it was this teaching in part that drove his daughter, Patti, to feel she was unworthy to the point of taking her own life.

"Once I began to realize and look at the real gay person in the real world versus what I had been taught, I realized how wrong what I have been taught was. And I really believe it's wrong. I believe a gay person can become a Christian and go to heaven just like a person who's not gay. That's what I believe now." Unfortunately for Mr. Mathis, his change was not enough to alter Patti's final decision.

Before Patti's death, she wrote a letter to her father which in part read, "[E]ven though I am not what you expected, and maybe the dreams you had for me are not my goals, I am still your daughter and I need your love, your respect, and your faith. And I promise you, Dad, regardless of how you see me or perceive my lifestyle, I am a part of you."

Mr. Mathis said, "You see what happens if you treat a child like I did—you scar that child and it's bound to bother that child's thought process. There's a possibility it could ruin them for life. I regret very much the mean things I said to Patti when I found out she was gay. And I realize now there was nothing wrong with Patti; something was wrong with me."

Mr. Mathis has been open and candid about his belief on the stance of religion and gays for some years now. He is quick to express that he feels the scars inflicted by religious groups and parents on gay or transgender children through their lack of support are lifelong and sometimes deadly. "I believe gay people are born from their mother's womb as gay. It is not a choice."

Mr. Mathis has stopped attending church, stating, "It has been a good long while since I have been." He struggles with the antiquated church belief that only non-gay people can go to heaven, and he states he cannot condone this behavior as a parishioner. He is a strong believer in God and the Bible and can and does quote it with ease in regular conversation, but he no longer believes in the discriminating, unsupportive ways of some organized religions.

What Does the Bible Say?

Recent Translations

The Bible does not address sexual orientation and gender identity specifically. It does, address the issue of men having sex with other men, but only in the context of acts of excess and lust, not with regard to love, and the context needs to be taken as a whole, not cherry-picked to suit one's point of view.

The Old Testament prohibits same sex relations, referring to it as an abomination. However, other passages speak to abominations as sexual intercourse with a woman during menstruation, eating rabbit, and shellfish, as well as charging interest on a loan. In today's culture, many of those so-called abominations are considered out-dated and are now ignored—all except gay relations. To some, this abomination should remain while others are, according to the ways of Christianity, foregone by grace with the New Testament.

The Old Testament also tells the story of Sodom and Gomorrah in which two angels were sent from heaven into the city disguised as men. The men of the city showed not only lack of hospitality to the strangers (hospitality being a strong biblical command) but threatened to rape the "angel men." God poured fire down on the city, destroying it and all of its inhabitants. Some would say that God destroyed the city due to its homosexual tendencies, while others would suggest that God destroyed the city because of the evil hearts and lack of hospitality to strangers by those in the city, which included those threatening gang rape on the angels-turned-men.

However, the New Testament holds the current ideology for Christians and is the book of grace. Jesus fulfilled the Old Testament, rendering its old laws obsolete and ending the law of righteousness, according to Hebrews 8:13 and Romans 10:4.

Paul, the author of the Book of Romans, condemned lustful and unnatural behavior. While many people consider same sex relationships "unnatural," Paul used the term "unnatural" to refer to things as trivial as men growing their hair long. "Unnatural" is also used in the Bible to refer to women who use *unnatural* powers (whatever they are), stating they shall be put to death. The word is also used to refer to men whose bodies are damaged or have an *unnatural* growth, saying they may not present an offering to God. And *unnatural* is used to describe a father having sexual relations with his son's wife, stating the two shall be put to death. The Bible also states those who are fornicators, idolaters, adulterers, or are guilty of *unnatural* crimes shall not inherit God's Kingdom. The word "unnatural" is used as a broad brushstroke with varying interpretations and beliefs.

Speaking to gay sexual orientation, most instances in biblical times were between master and slave, between adult men and adolescent boys, and in the form of prostitution. And many of the men who perpetrated the gay behavior were married to women. Therefore, one could argue that Paul was referring to the lustful, excessive behavior of the sexual acts of that time, not to those in loving, committed, and faithful same-sex relationships; those types of loving relationships are not addressed. It should also be noted that in both the Old and New Testaments, same-gender sexual relationships are condemned because of power imbalance. We would also, today, condemn sex with a child or with someone in slavery, or forcing someone to have sex because of a job.

Older Translations

While writing this book, a dear friend of mine, who also happens to be a gay man and a former Catholic priest, led me to an article by Ed Oxford, a gay Christian graduate of Talbot School of Theology and a researcher in how the Bible has been weaponized against LGBTQ+ people. This is a complicated journey, but one that needs to be told to invoke thought and contemplation.

The word "homosexual" first appeared in the Revised Standard Version (RSV) of the Bible published in 1946 (the New Testament was first published in 1946 with the Old Testament in 1952; the New Testament was again revised in 1971). The RSV is an English translation of the Bible published by the Division of Christian Education of the National Council of Churches (NCC). The RSV is a revision of the American Standard Version and was intended to be a readable and literally accurate modern English translation, which aimed to "preserve all that is best in the English Bible as it has been known and used through the centuries" and "to put the message of the Bible in simple, enduring words that are worthy to stand in the great Tyndale-King James tradition."[29] Mr. Oxford and his team set out to understand how other cultures and translations treated the most used anti-gay versus (Leviticus, Timothy, and Corinthians) when they were translated during the Reformation 500 years ago. The team gathered Bibles from multiple languages, French, German, Irish, Gaelic, Czechoslovakian and Polish, as far back as possible.

It should be pointed out that "homosexual" was a word created by Germans and made famous by Karl Friedrich Otto Westphal, a German psychiatrist from Berlin in his 1870 article, "Contrary Sexual Feeling," which is coined the terminology for the categorization of sexual orientation.[30] Given that the Germans were the creators of the word "homosexual," it would stand to reason that the German translation of the Bible should be the first one to use it. However, that is not the case.

Oxford's research showed that the German Bible from the 1800s show in Leviticus 18:22 the English translation says, "Man shall not lie with man, for it is an abomination," but the German version says, "Man shall not lie with young boys as he does with a woman, for it is an abomination." Leviticus 20:13 also refers to "young boys." In this same translation, 1 Corinthians translated *arsenokoitai* (which is the original Greek word used in the Bible), which says, "Boy molesters will not inherit the kingdom of God."

So, what does this really mean? This means there are some discrepancies in translations, as well as some possible influence from different cultures regarding these translations. Oxford and his team then moved on to a copy of Martin Luther's original German translation of the Bible from 1534. Luther (1483–1546) was a German professor of theology, a composer, priest, monk, and seminal figure in the Protestant Reformation. He came to reject several teachings and practices of the Roman Catholic Church, in particular he disputed the view on indulgences. In Luther's translation from 1534, the word in question used was *knabenschander*: *knaben* meaning boy and *schander* meaning molester. This translation or *knabenschander* was carried through for the next several centuries of German Bible translations with *knabenschander* also being found in 1 Timothy.

The team then searched to see if the word *arsenokoitai* was changed to homosexual in modern translation, and they found that the first time "homosexual" appeared in German translation was in 1983. This news did not sit well with the researchers, given the influence the Germans previously had regarding the researchers' view on homosexuality, so they dug deeper. What they found was that the American company Biblica, which publishes the NIV Bible (New

International Version), paid for the 1983 German translation of the Bible. Thus, according to Oxford and his research team, Biblica and/ or its translators, may well have influenced the decision to use the word "homosexual" in the German Bible. Oxford states, regarding the translation, "I think there is a gay agenda after all!"[31]

Oxford and his team continued their research, finding that a 1674 Swedish translation and an 1830 Norwegian translation of the Bible uses the terms "boy abusers" and "boy molesters." Reading these translations, Oxford states that the ancient world condoned and encouraged a system whereby young boys (ages approximately eight through twelve) were coupled with older men. This system was used by parents to advance their sons in society. Thereby, according to Oxford, most translations thought these verses were obviously referring to pederasty, not homosexuality.[32]

Oxford's team used the data available to them from old libraries, finding lexicons from 1483, to look up *arsenokoitai*, which gave the Latin equivalents of *paedico* and *praedico*, meaning *pederasty* or *knabenschander* ("boy molester" in German). Martin Luther was born in 1483, so he would have used such a lexicon. This lexicon would have used information from the previous 1000-plus years that included information passed down from church fathers.

The result of the inconsistencies in translation has likely become the platform for many to declare that "homosexuality is abomination" and "the Bible says homosexuality is a sin." But is that what the Bible really said? In order to make an educated decision, we must look farther than the ten-second blurbs on social media and the person behind the podium who may not have looked deep enough into the subject. I would encourage those standing on principle to look beyond the past seventy years of biblical publication.

A Matter of Conscience?

In Idaho, there has been a fourteen-year human rights fight regarding the Add the Words campaign. Add the Words is the name of a political action committee to add four words to the Idaho Human Rights Act, "sexual orientation" and "gender identity." The four words being requested would, according to the Add the Words nonprofit organization, enable "all Idahoans to be free, live and thrive without fear of discrimination, domination and violence."

Idaho, or at least its legislative body, seems to take great exception to allowing equality for gay, queer, and transgender people. The state's Human Rights Act bans discrimination in employment, housing, and public accommodations on the basis of race, gender, religion, age or disability *but does not cover discrimination based on sexual orientation or gender identity.* What that means is that in Idaho, people can legally be fired from their job, evicted from their home, or denied services and accommodation because they are gay or transgender. At the time of this writing there were only fourteen municipalities in the State of Idaho that had bypassed the state and approved their own anti-discrimination ordinances.

It would appear that the biggest pushback to this equality/anti-discrimination act is coming from a group of people who think that being forced *not* to discriminate against LGBTQ+ persons would go against their religious beliefs. It seems that if you do not belong to the *chosen* religious culture or *look* and *act* in the way those people think is "correct" and "normal," you are not respected, not equal, and not worthy of Idaho's governmental protection.

A recent speaker in favor of Add the Words was Reverend Dr. Andrew Kukla of the First Presbyterian Church Boise, who spoke on behalf of the Interfaith Equality Coalition. Kukla's comments were directed largely toward a particular senator who has always stood in opposition to Add the Words. This senator has stated, "Nobody wants discrimination, but there are fears out there that we need to address on both sides." He has additionally stated, "[C]oncerns remain that affording protections to LGBTQ+ persons could jeopardize others' religious freedoms and rights of conscience."

Rev. Kukla, during a speech addressing this subject, said:

> We take deep exception when [this senator] seems to speak for all people of faith when he makes the claim that Add the Words and faith have two different agendas. When he presents the false dichotomy that equality is opposed to religious freedom. Or that religious freedom is opposed to equality.
>
> I would remind [this senator] that churches have not been good at equality. Churches doubled down on slavery. Churches remain places of deep racial distrust. Churches remain places that force my female colleagues to put clergy collars on just so that they don't have to explain they really are clergy. Churches have been on the backside of equality forever and the Add the Words issue is no different. We still haven't learned.
>
> He [the senator] represents a faith and speaks that it is all faiths, but it is a small sliver of one particular faith. A particular faith that has chosen to take a few small biblical texts that are relatively obscure in meaning and translation and read them over and against the entire witness of scripture which says again and again, to love your neighbor as yourself.

*Not just your neighbor, but the stranger, the resident alien ...
I actually don't care what [this senator] thinks of us: his faith
demands that he care equally for people he does and doesn't
like. When Jesus says, in the Second Commandment, "You
shall love your neighbor as yourself," he put no conditions on
neighbor. None.*

*[This senator] represents a faith that continues to want to
double down on those conditions, and they have no place in
religious rhetoric. So, while [this senator] and the majority
continue to have power and continue to ask those who are
oppressed to compromise with the poor people in power who
can't handle to lose, it isn't his faith he is being asked to compromise, it is the particular representation of a hate and a fear.
He is deeply afraid of you, of us. And that's what he's asking
you to compromise. And the answer to that is, we won't.*

To further address the senator's concerns about protecting
Idahoan's religious freedoms, the following is a good representation
of how protected Idaho's religious freedoms really are:

- Idaho currently has a robust religious freedom exemption
  specifically protecting people from discrimination based on
  their religion.
- Idaho's Constitution states no person can use religion or
  religious liberty as a reason to justify "pernicious practices" or
  do harm to others.
- The current Idaho Human Rights Act already bans
  discrimination based on race, color, *religion* [emphasis added],
  sex, national origin, age, and disability.

- Idaho's Human Rights Act balances civil rights with religious liberty with the help of the Human Rights Commission to investigate and mediate in order to protect individuals and businesses in cases of alleged discrimination.
- Even today some Americans hold religious beliefs based on the Bible's ideas about slavery and interracial marriage. Yet when *race* was included in Idaho's civil rights and human rights acts, religious freedom exemptions were not created to allow people who held these religious beliefs to continue to discriminate by depriving black Americans of their freedoms or by refusing to provide wedding-related services to interracial couples.
- Many religions deny women the right to own property, marry freely, or exercise other basic civil liberties. Yet when *sex* was included in Idaho's civil rights and human rights laws, religious exemptions were not created to allow people to continue to deprive women of their basic freedoms or prohibit them from accessing goods, services or other public accommodations.
- The first sentence of the Idaho Constitution addresses public accommodation and lists acquiring property among our inalienable rights as individuals. A religious exemption permitting people to refuse to provide gay or transgender people with wedding related goods and services would violate Idaho's Constitution.
- If Idaho created an exemption allowing religious people to continue to discriminate against gay and transgender people this would unconstitutionally prioritize in law one religious belief over the beliefs of other religions—those which place priority and belief that gay and transgender people are made in the image of God and deserving of full liberties and inclusion under existing law.[33]

Denying the inclusion of "sexual orientation" and "gender

identity" sends a strong message that those in the LGBTQ+ community are not fully human, not worthy of protection, respect, love, dignity, services, and accommodations. It shows they cannot and should not be allowed employment, housing, and shelter and that it is okay to oppress yet another community of individuals because of what others feel as "not normal."

A final thought for Christians:

> *If you are Christian, ask yourself, "What would Jesus do?" Would Jesus say you should refuse to bake the wedding cake for your neighbors? How do we define what celebrating or participation in a wedding is? Is that just making a wedding bouquet and taking photographs or is it renting the wedding gown, the tuxedo or the hall? Selling the paper napkins? Growing the flowers for the bouquets? Fixing the newlywed's broken car? Renting them their hotel room on their honeymoon? Renting an apartment to their family? Schooling their children? Serving them an anniversary dinner? Allowing them to live in a retirement community? Accommodating the funeral when one of them passes away?*[34]

As Christians, it is important to utilize the vast resources available to us to sift through the religious writings and opinions to reveal where modern society and religion should stand regarding gay and transgender persons. It should also be remembered that excerpting certain text from any publication can lead to misappropriation to achieve any nefarious goal.

Doing nothing is also unacceptable. By doing nothing and

being apathetic, believing it "isn't about you," or that it doesn't affect you, you are allowing inequality, discrimination, and lack of inclusion to live in your own backyard. Without protection, gay and transgender people are at a far higher risk of suicide, homelessness, joblessness, and violence.

The life you save by standing up could be that of your own child.

CHAPTER 6
Playing Politics with Peoples' Lives

BASIC HUMAN AND CIVIL RIGHTS for the LGBTQ+ community begin with laws that require the prosecution of crimes that discriminate against members of the community and extend to LGBTQ+ people equal treatment—including fair housing and employment, uninhibited travel and voting, the right to marry whom they choose, and adopt children. And as with sexual and racial discrimination patterns in the United States, legislating to protect the LGBTQ+ community is only part of the process, but it's a critical step that acknowledges and documents those rights.

Widespread social acceptance of those rights will take longer. And until that happens, every gay and transgender child (one of whom could be your child), every day at school, will be fearful of using the restroom, will dread the showers during gym class, and will avoid little-used hallways in case they are attacked. And every gay and transgender adult will struggle to find and keep housing and employment and be paid a fair and equal wage. They will continue to face hardships when it comes to healthcare and everyday services, and possibly become or remain isolated because of continued harassment and threats.

Less than half of the states in America have laws regarding anti-discrimination of LGBTQ+ persons; Representative John McCrostie's home state of Idaho is one of those states without anti-discrimination laws. McCrostie has fought for the Add the Words campaign (discussed in the previous chapter) for years to get "sexual orientation" and "gender identity" added to the state's Human Rights Act. Statewide, only 14 out of the 201 municipalities have adopted LGBTQ+ anti-discrimination ordinances.

McCrostie—a married gay man—lives in Garden City, a small community nestled between the two largest cities in Idaho, Boise, and Meridian. Both Boise and Meridian have passed anti-discrimination ordinances but Garden City has not. What this means to McCrostie and others in the LGBTQ+ community living in Garden City is they are protected from discrimination and harassment when visiting either neighboring municipality—but not when they cross the street to go back home. Discrimination against them for their sexual orientation or gender identity is lawful in Garden City, as it is in most other places in the United States.

In McCrostie's words:

> *I am an educator, a lawyer, and an elected state lawmaker. I work with Democrats and Republicans, progressives and conservatives. I fight to ensure that Idaho children get the best education possible so they can pursue whatever dreams they can imagine. I am a husband. I am a lifelong Idahoan. I play in a few bands. I am also gay. In Idaho, I can be fired*

> *from my job or denied housing just for that reason. Although the word "law" exists in two of my titles, Idaho law does not protect all of my American freedoms and liberties.*[35]

McCrostie feels that the Add the Words legislation has not passed for three reasons. First, the citizens who have testified in favor of the Act were not necessarily from districts where legislators' votes needed swaying. In other words, the legislators could discount the testimony of members of the public because it was not reflective of those who resided in their district. In order to help pass this legislation, McCrostie believes more people from all parts of the state need to speak out in favor of it.

Second, McCrostie believes there was pushback from businesses who did not want to provide services to same-sex couples for their marriage ceremonies. He said there did not seem to be opposition to anti-discrimination regarding employment, housing, or education; however, businesses that would be required to accommodate same-sex marriages (the florist, the cake baker, the photographer, and so on) were possibly opposed to this. His takeaway was that people did not feel they should be required to serve gay couples if that conflicted with their religious or moral views.

Third, McCrostie saw the bathroom rights of transgender persons as a stumbling block. The transgender bathroom issue revolves around which bathroom transgender people should be allowed to use; the one which reflects their gender assignment at birth or their current gender identity. McCrostie feels that *fear* is the driving force behind this contentious debate. He said testimony from the transgender population argued that while they felt they should be allowed to use the bathroom that reflects their identity, they were fearful of their safety using *either* gender's public restrooms. McCrostie stated he heard that most transgender persons would prefer a non-designated, single-door bathroom for anyone to use, regardless of their gender identity. I personally prefer those types of bathrooms as well.

Public Restroom Battleground

THIS IS CERTAINLY NOT THE first time civil rights issues focused on the use of public bathrooms. In 1864, following the Civil War and the ratification of the Thirteenth Amendment that abolished slavery, most of the states of the former Confederacy states adopted "black codes"—laws that were similar to former slave laws. The intent of these codes was to limit or restrict African Americans' movements and force them into a labor economy based on low wages and debt.[36]

The black codes laid the foundation for the system of laws and customs supporting a system of white supremacy that would be known as Jim Crow laws. Jim Crow laws were statutes and ordinances established between 1874 and 1975 to separate the white and black races in the American South. In theory, it was to create "separate but equal" treatment, but in practice, Jim Crow laws condemned black citizens to inferior treatment and facilities. Education was segregated, as were public facilities, hotels, and restaurants. Jim Crow laws led to treatment and accommodations that were almost always inferior to those provided to white Americans.[37]

The most important and infamous Jim Crow laws required that

public schools, public facilities (water fountains and toilets) and public transportation have separate facilities for whites and blacks. These discriminatory laws required black people to

- attend separate schools and churches;
- use public bathrooms marked "for colored only";
- eat in a separate section of a restaurant; and
- sit in the rear of the bus.

This type of segregation is referred to as "fate control" in interpersonal social psychology. Fate control is the ability of person A to influence person B, no matter what person B does or "Put them in their place," according to Rupert W. Nacoste, PhD, Professor of Psychology at North Carolina State University.[38]

Dr. Nacoste likens fate control to a form of interpersonal power that can show up in the form of institutional power—for example, government. Nacoste's example of institutional power refers to a 2016 piece of legislation (North Carolina's HB2), which is based on transgender persons having to use the bathroom of the gender to which they were born, not to which they identify.

Nacoste says this legislation was not just about the bathroom. As with the Civil Rights Act of 1965, which was well known for being at least in part about segregated bathrooms, this legislation was about the bigger picture. The Civil Rights Act was about equal protection under the law, protection against government support of prejudice, bigotry, and discrimination. Just as with the bathroom issue for black people, there is a much bigger issue at stake for transgender people than a toilet.

According to Dr. Nacoste, the Jim Crow laws of racial segregation regarding the bathroom was such a heated issue because, "If you have to use the same bathrooms, then at the most basic level you cannot say you are a better, a more important, or a more authentic citizen or human." That, he says, is why it was so important that African Americans waged and won their fight to remove the stigma and laws that allowed white citizens to "show them their place."[39]

"NC HB2 legislation is institutional use of fate control to support fear of and other anti-group feelings toward transgender people; that is heterosexism," stated Dr. Nacoste. "[This] legislation is not about bathrooms. [It] is about resisting social changes that extend equal protection under the law to transgendered people."

Serving in the U.S. Armed Forces

THE U.S. MILITARY AND ITS politics have substantially flip-flopped regarding the LGBTQ+ community. In preparation for WWII, psychiatric screening became part of the induction process, and the then-current psychiatric view of "homosexuality" as an indicator of psychopathology was introduced into military regulations.[40]

Due to shortages of soldiers during WWII, the Korean War, and the Vietnam War, the "mental defect" claim, which barred gays from serving in the military, was relaxed and in some cases lifted. However, when the shortage of military personnel was no longer an issue, gay servicemen would be summarily discharged from duty.

The U.S. military has been known to be discriminatory throughout its history. Native Americans were not granted citizenship until 1924, so until that time, they fought in U.S. military conflicts for reasons other than simply serving the United States. In WWI, with the need for soldiers, Native Americans were offered U.S. citizenships in exchange for their enlistment.

Segregation of African American soldiers and nurses in the U.S. armed forces remained in effect until an Executive Order by President Harry S. Truman was signed in 1948. It wasn't until 1954, however, that the last all-black unit was disbanded. African Americans may have been able to serve in the military as an equal, but they were not allowed to fully participate in voting rights throughout the United States until 1965.

Chris T. was in the U.S. Navy during this volatile time for gays. Chris knew he was gay, but he also knew he could never come out to his peers, as he would be discharged from service. He told me, "If they found out you were gay or even suspected it, you would be investigated. They would show you Polaroids of naked women and ask you, 'Does this do anything for you?' If you passed this test, then you would need a witness or a chaplain to corroborate your status. If you didn't pass these tests, you were thrown out of the service, just like that."

Chris remained a closeted gay during his entire tenure in the navy. Perhaps even worse for Chris was that during this time, he met and fell in love with a man who he believes may have been his soul mate. Unfortunately, due to the fear of both men being involuntarily discharged if found out, he never acted on his feelings, and they ended up getting stationed in different ports. Over time, the two lost track of each other and Chris has spent the last several decades wondering about and looking for his lost love.

In 1982, the Department of Defense completely banned gays from the military, stating that "homosexuality was incompatible with military service." According to a 1992 report, nearly 17,000 men and women were discharged under that directive.[41]

In 1993, the "Don't Ask, Don't Tell, Don't Pursue" policy was enacted. This policy stated that a person's sexual preference would not be questioned and a person would not be discharged merely for being gay. They would, however, be involuntarily discharged if they spoke of their sexual orientation, showed public displays of affection or had sexual relations with members of the same sex. This policy was repealed in late 2010, and service members could serve without fear of discharge for being gay.

Until 2016, there was a ban on openly transgender persons serving in the military. The ban on transgender persons serving in the military was again sought through legislation one year later, in July 2017; an injunction by the higher courts has paused this ban. In 2018, the U.S. Administration altered course slightly and sought to ban all transgender persons from the military except under *certain limited circumstances*, stating that persons with a history or diagnosis of gender dysphoria present considerable risk to military effectiveness.

In 2013, the Department of Defense made available to all spouses of same-sex marriages (with proof of a valid, legal marriage) the same benefits in place for those in straight marriages. At the time of writing this book, that policy is still in effect.

This regulatory history shows that progress can be made— however, the military still does not have a fully egalitarian policy.

Family Laws: Marriage and Adoption

ONGOING DEBATES AND CONTROVERSY SURROUND same-sex marriage, both in the U.S. and internationally. The United States has gone back and forth, declaring it legal or not legal, predominately based on fundamentalist religious contentions that the union should be between one man and one woman. In some countries, same-sex marriage is criminal, not recognized at all, or can lead to death if uncovered. Other countries have made same-sex marriage legal.

Adoption is another difficult road made harder by differing laws and regulations throughout the United States and internationally. Adoption for same-sex couples is not legal in many states, and in states where it is legal, restrictions and difficulties are much greater for these couples than for straight couples. In certain states, only one person in a same-sex relationship can be considered the adoptive parent. And only some states will allow the other person to come alongside later and become a legal parent through second-parent or stepparent adoption.

If this same-sex couple splits up, the second parent (the nonlegal, nonbiological parent) generally has no rights if there is no stepparent adoption in place. Many courts will treat the second parent as a nonparent and will not enforce rights of any kind with the child, including visitation.

To even further muddy these already dark waters, if a same-sex couple who adopts a child then moves to a state where same-sex relationships are not recognized, there could be further negative implications to the nonlegal or nonbiological parent, if a second parent or stepparent adoption is not in place. The second parent may not be recognized at all regarding legal, medical, religious, or school-related decisions.

Families and spouses of same-sex couples are also seeing some new restrictions that will hinder their lives and marginalize them further. It was reported in October 2018 that a new U.S. State Department regulation states it will only recognize marriages, not same-sex partnerships, when granting diplomatic visas to partners. This change will affect approximately 105 families in the U.S., including fifty-five that are here with international organizations. Given that only twenty-five countries allow same-sex marriages, very few of those individuals who are in these same-sex relationships are from countries where same-sex marriage is legal.[42] Therefore many of the partners and families will no longer be granted diplomatic visas, meaning families could be separated and forced to live apart. This too could bring retaliation from their country of origin, if the reason behind the rejected visa is discovered.

Chris and Andy were forced to fly across the country in order to be legally married. They were unable to have their family and friends witness their union because of the exorbitant expense of marrying 3,000 miles away from home. They would also like a family one day but find the hoops they will have to jump through daunting and discouraging.

Chris is an American Sign Language interpreter, and Andy is finishing his residency to become a physician. As a young, highly educated couple, they fully realize the difficulties they are facing in adopting. They have regular discussions on where they will live once Andy is done with his schooling, a decision based on what states recognize gay adoptions, or alternatively what states have laws that protect the "adoptive" parent as well as the "second" parent.

My son would like a family one day too and has become an advocate for adoption. He is not interested in having children of his own but wants to take in and care for children who have no other home; a truly admirable decision by any account. However, being gay means he will have many more hurdles to jump than a straight man in order to create his desired family.

Rebekah and Sue lived as a married couple for many, many years before actually being legally married, as marriage for two women was not recognized until very recently. They had a commitment ceremony in 2000 in New Mexico and then had a legal marriage performed in Portland, Oregon in 2012 when it became legal. Unfortunately, this marriage was only legal for six weeks. They received in the mail their original check with notification that the Supreme Court had overturned its ruling on gay marriage. Years later, in 2016, Rebekah and Sue married again, this time in Seattle, Washington. So far, that marriage is still considered legal.

When Rebekah and Sue decided to have a child, their path was equally bumpy. They initially asked a friend if he would be a sperm donor but ultimately used a sperm-bank donor through California. Sue tried thirteen times to become pregnant but complications were abundant, leaving the couple to make the decision to implant Sue's viable embryo into Rebekah. They now share a lovely young daughter together. It should be noted that Sue was required to legally terminate her biological parental rights to the embryo that ultimately became her daughter because of the laws—or lack thereof—regarding same-sex parents. Sue has since filed legal documents to allow her to be the co-parent or second parent to her own child.

Through all of this, however, neither Rebekah nor Sue lost their sense of humor, telling a story of one of their intrauterine inseminations. They had to drive from Seattle, where they were living, to Tacoma to pick up the sperm and were told to keep it warm. Rebekah in all her wisdom and good humor nestled the tube containing what would hopefully one day become their child, between her breasts: "The warmest place I could think of," she said.

She then looked at Sue and said, "We could save a lot of money if we just go home and use the turkey baster!"

Legislating for "Religious Freedom"

THE STATE OF TEXAS, KNOWN for everything big, went big with its 2018 Republican platform, which included new language on religious freedom for business owners. Its platform opposed "any law that required any private business or individual to create or provide a custom product or service, or any kind of expressive work, or enter into a contract, or be coerced into any speech that is not their own," obviously referring to vendors who do not want to provide services to same-sex couples. Thus, this platform encouraged inequality and condoned discrimination.

This platform goes on to state, with regard to transgender issues, "We oppose all efforts to validate transgender identity" and continues by saying that transgender persons should not serve in the military as a special class and no special considerations or medical treatment should be required or offered.

Further, the platform added, "We urge the complete repeal of the Hate Crimes Law since ample laws are currently in effect to punish criminal behavior towards other persons."[43]

Regarding this platform, the *Houston Chronicle* reported that some younger delegates got the party to remove the following statement: "Homosexual behavior is contrary to the fundamental truths that have been ordained by God in the Bible."

Freedom of Movement: ID Cards and Passports

ON NATIONAL AND INTERNATIONAL LEVELS, the LGBTQ+ community is embroiled in political controversy regarding travel, marriage, and overall safety. New rules and regulations are being enacted that make it more difficult for transgender people to travel. Hate crimes in some countries are ignored or pushed aside if perpetrated against gay and transgender people. These acts of violence, in some cases, are not considered crimes at all but rather a "duty" to rid the world of LGBTQ+ persons.

LGBTQ+ persons are encouraged to check the level of acceptance in a country prior to travel. The U.S. Department of State—Bureau of Consular Affairs has a website where up-to-date information can be found. That site with its specific section for LGBTI (I = intersex) travelers is located at **travel.state.gov/content/travel/en/international-travel/before-you-go/travelers-with-special-considerations/lgbti.html.** Within this site, you can search each country or region you desire to visit and scroll to find the specific section for LGBTI travelers where that country's laws and customs are explained as they relate to LGBTI persons. These warnings need to be taken seriously.

Drew, a non-binary person who has had FTM (female to male) "top surgery," is in a quandary regarding government-approved identifications. Drew was able to change their name on their driver's license when they transitioned but not their gender, because they have not undergone a full transition, and never will. Therefore, Drew identifies as non-binary.

Drew is afraid they will not be able to get a passport because of the gender identification restriction and doesn't know if their birth certificate can be changed. Drew stated that they identify more as male than as female but would prefer there to be a non-binary gender category. That option, however, is only available in a few states; Drew's is not one of them. Drew simply self-identifies as a person, not a specific gender, and feels that the government is making things very difficult for transgender people due to the new regulation for gender identity to be a person's birth assignment *unless they are fully physically transitioned* (full top and bottom surgery). And even the possibility of acknowledging surgically transitioned gender is now in question.

Drew is in a true quagmire regarding legal identification. They cannot get a passport because their birth certificate still states "female" and cites a "dead" female name, yet their driver's license states "male" and uses their male name of Drew. Therefore, the Drews of the world are restricted in their travel due to their gender identity.

Political Leaders Affect Social Acceptance

ALL THOSE I SPOKE WITH while researching this book felt that the political climate, at the time of writing, has promoted more hate toward the LGBTQ+ community because of the attitudes of political leaders.

"I was a Republican for a long time," Rebekah said. She is a married lesbian in an ultra-conservative state. "I used to think I was socially liberal and fiscally conservative. [Now] I don't think you can separate the two. I think if you are going to help other people you are all in or you are not. So, I am a flaming liberal," she said, laughing.

Chris D. didn't discuss his preferred political party but instead expressed how hurtful it was that his family voted for leaders who have been openly hateful toward the LGBTQ+ community. He said that when leaders openly express dislike for gay people, such hostile behavior becomes socially acceptable for others to emulate. He has observed a negative shift in affirmative acceptance since the latest election.

Patti Mathis took her own life as a very young person. She felt bullied and unaccepted as a lesbian, according to her father, William Mathis. Mr. Mathis blames part of this feeling of unacceptance on the world's leaders. "People who are elected have a responsibility to make this place a better place to live in. They need to stop and look at all this hate and rhetoric because other people listen. We need to try to make this a better place, not a worse place," said Mr. Mathis.

Mr. Mathis went on to quote the Declaration of Independence, "We hold these truths to be self-evident, that all men are created equal, that they are endowed by their Creator with certain unalienable Rights, that among these are Life, Liberty, and the pursuit of Happiness. And that statement does not exclude gay people, it *includes* gay people. So we need to realize that and treat gay people accordingly."

Mr. Mathis became an instant media figure when he protested against politicians who were "lambasting gay people." He said while he knew they were not speaking of his daughter directly, they were speaking about her, regardless. He said he could not sit quietly and listen, so he wrote a sign against their defamatory commentary and went on a one-man march to get his point out. "I am not a hero; I was just a father mad about a politician saying bad things about my daughter, even though he didn't call my daughter by name," Mr. Mathis said.

My son Hunter agrees with Mr. Mathis, and says, "You are part of the problem if you sit by and silently let the politicians bash us."

My friend Carolyn has courage. She does not sit quietly by; instead, she stands up for her friends and strangers in the LGBTQ+ community. In a recent speech she gave at a city council meeting in her hometown, she told the members that they needed to do the right thing toward people who are LGBTQ+, regardless of their own feelings.

She told the council:

> By adopting this nondiscrimination ordinance, the city will be sending a clear message of inclusivity and tolerance to our youth and more. You have an opportunity to make a compassionate decision and to proclaim this city as one that values and welcomes all people. We cannot legislate kindness, but we can provide a measure of safety and a message that we will not tolerate hate.
>
> I am asking you tonight as a person of faith and resident of this city to vote in favor of the nondiscrimination ordinance. Kindness and safety are values that all religions hold in common. Voting in favor of this ordinance does not infringe on the rights of people's faith practices. Instead, it highlights the place where all religions meet—compassion.

With the help and voices of allies like Carolyn, the anti-discrimination ordinance passed, 4–2.

In my community, a city ordinance referred to as the Open Carry Law was adopted. Essentially, this means anyone can legally carry a registered firearm in plain sight—as opposed to concealing it. Recently, an incident was published in local news media that highlighted some of the ramifications of this ordinance. I am neither a fan nor an opponent of this, but I came across a post from a local transgender woman and wanted to share a different perspective on how discrimination looks and feels:

> *Recently [a state representative] was confronted by a business owner when the representative and his friends were trying to get a sandwich while openly carrying weapons. I sent the representative the following email just now.*
>
> *Representative,*
>
> *Regarding the incident where you and your friends were confronted [for openly carrying firearms in a restaurant] and made to feel uncomfortable and unwelcome. You were all just being your authentic selves and you were discriminated against based on how you looked and who you are. You were denied services in a public place and that must have hurt. All because of who you are; your identity went against the owner's sincerely held beliefs.*
>
> *That is something thousands of [us] who happen to be lesbian, gay, bisexual, or transgender face every day. Judgment, exclusion, discrimination, fear. Imagine if that discrimination meant that your access to a job, or housing, or medical care, or services was at stake. Imagine how powerless you would feel. How you would feel unable to protect or provide for your family. This, representative, is what Adding the Words "sexual orientation" and "gender identity" to our [state's] human*

rights act is all about. Except you can conceal or remove some-thing that made you stand out. For you it honestly is a choice and not how you inherently are.

~ Dianne Piggott

There is a definite need for politics in any society, but when the politicians are not well behaved, the best we can hope for is that people will step up and lead with kindness, equality, and love. The countrywide epidemic of loud, self-serving politicians in the United States seems to be showcasing misbehavior.

CHAPTER 7
Fearing the "Other"

IT IS MY CONTENTION THAT under-education and fear are the driving forces behind discrimination. A person who does not have the tools to empathize or appreciate another person's difference can feel their way of life is being threatened by what they perceive as an agenda against them. They may also feel intimidated or oppressed by difference. This under-education can turn to fear, which in turn can lead to aggression or violence.

The broadcast and online news, while often sensationalized to make a story, is riddled with fear-inducing stories that can lead people to misunderstand a culture or person. Hate crimes can certainly be the product of the biased opinions that have been disseminated and held as truth by those listening.

We were taught from the time we were small to listen to and respect those in power and to believe what they say and do as they instruct. These politicians are, after all, our leaders and presumably our protectors. If those in power hold a disdain for a certain group or way of life, then those who adhere to the teachings of "respect those in authority and power" will unquestioningly behave and act accordingly. In our current political climate, it is easy to see how the discrimination against and violence toward LGBTQ+ persons has ramped up.

As discussed already, religion is another fear generator. For Islamic states, where orthodox Muslims claim that the Hadith literature contains the authentic sayings of Muhammad, the belief is that being gay is sinful and a perverted deviation from the norm. This belief is held across all Islamic schools of thought and is a punishable offense. The punishment differs in each region from no physical punishment, to severe punishment, to execution.

I do not want to become embroiled in a religious debate over right and wrong and biblical prose regarding LGBTQ+. However, I have read the Bible several times, and I think it is thoroughly disingenuous for Christian-professing believers to not appreciate that this marginalized community is the proverbial *least of these* who Christians are instructed to care for, stand up for, and love; not just put on a forced smile and feign tolerance. And my question to those throwing the Bible at LGBTQ+ persons is, *Who are you to judge?* "Only if you have removed the plank from your eye do you have the right to speak of the speck in someone else's eye" (NIV, Matthew 7:1-5).

Chera Kelsey, MSW (Master of Social Work), whose work is intertwined with LGBTQ+ youth, explained that she has seen a lack of education and fear play a part in her work with foster families. She has seen families become unwilling or unable to work with or house youths of the LGBTQ+ community due to numerous reasons, including fear and religion. She said those who identify as LGBTQ+ definitely have a more difficult time being placed and finding permanency in the system.

Chera said she can appreciate how a person's faith, religion, and spirituality is so intimate, personal, and ingrained in them that it complicates how they may see people in a marginalized community. She agreed that fear plays a large part in discrimination, and she has seen the results of that discrimination: depression, feelings of unworthiness, self-harm, and large rates of attempted suicide.

The struggle to discover our own intellectual understanding, innermost feelings, and spiritual beliefs as they relate to the LGBTQ+ community can be daunting. But the truth is we don't need to understand *everything*—we just need to understand that respecting other people does not mean only your straight neighbor or only situations you have experienced for yourself.

Understanding without Separation

WHY ARE SO MANY PEOPLE upset by gay and transgender people? I have heard some whispered conversations about noticing a lot of young people "turning" gay. And in other circles, I have heard people state that being gay is "trendy." Gay, like transgender, is neither a fad nor a contagion. You do not simply *become* gay or transgender.

I remember when one of my sons (not Hunter) told me he and his best friend were going to their eighth-grade dance in dresses. I laughed. I thought it was funny but told him to make sure he didn't get in trouble doing it. He told me they had made arrangements with their favorite math teacher to take a few minutes out of class to change before the in-school dance. The boys had it all planned—they were going to shave their legs and underarms, had borrowed dresses, and enlisted the help of some girls with makeup artistry skills, and had purchased balloons to wear as breasts; a little over the top, perhaps (no pun intended).

I saw no problem with any of this until I got a call from the school saying I needed to pick up my son for wearing a dress at school. I had to take time off work and drive thirty minutes to the school. When I got there, I was anything but pleased. I marched into the administrator's office and asked what was going on.

"Look at these two, that's what's going on," the principal said to me.

"What's wrong with them? I think they look cute," I said.

"You are okay with this?" he asked incredulously.

"Okay with what?" I said.

"Okay with them wearing dresses," the principal said.

"I am okay with it. I knew they were doing it," I explained.

The principal told me it was inappropriate for them to be wearing dresses and they needed to leave the school grounds, as they were going to be expelled. I am not sure if I literally held my hand up to stop the principal or if I simply want to believe I did. Regardless, I did ask specifically why it was inappropriate and on what grounds would they be expelled.

"Boys are not allowed to wear dresses to school," he said.

"And where in the student handbook does it say that?" I asked. I do specifically recall adding, "And does the handbook also say that girls are not allowed to wear pants? Because if boys can't wear dresses then girls shouldn't be allowed to wear pants."

"No, the handbook doesn't say either. It is just inappropriate," he insisted.

"I'm sorry, I disagree. If you can't prove to me there is something written that specifically says boys cannot wear dresses to school, then we have nothing further to talk about. And these boys will not be expelled!" I said.

Somewhere in this I also reminded the principal that I worked for an attorney and the last thing he wanted was a harassment or discrimination suit brought because two boys wore a dress to school. I even mentioned contacting the ACLU (American Civil Liberties Union) if he was going to discriminate against these boys.

"Well, the dresses themselves are inappropriate." The principal made a last-ditch effort to win his point.

"How so?" I asked.

"They have spaghetti straps and those are not allowed."

"I can appreciate that," I said. "So what would you do if a girl wore spaghetti straps to school?" I asked.

"She would have to change or go home and put something different on," he said.

"Fine," I said to the principal, then turned to the boys and said, "Boys, go change out of your spaghetti straps. And don't wear spaghetti straps to school again."

The boys sheepishly left to change out of the dresses. I am not sure if they were timid because of everything that had happened or specifically because a crazy-sounding mom threatened to level charges of discrimination against their school. I then turned to the principal and said something along the lines of, "I assume we have nothing further to discuss." I left, and the boys were not expelled.

Little did I know then that I was standing up for the rights of people who identified differently than the societal norm. I have never forgotten this, nor has my son. I was his hero that day because I did right by him. I stood up for him, and he never forgot it.

Did he *turn* transgender because of his brief moment cross-dressing?

No. Was I afraid he was going to transition into the opposite gender because of this? Never even crossed my mind. Looking back at this incident, I believe that because I didn't put my children in gender-specific roles or a "heterosexual" box, they felt comfortable to be who they were, where they were.

It's not my intention to set up my own parenting experience as a standard, and I feel blessed that my son Hunter came through his self-realization and his coming out as well as he did. I followed my heart and did what I thought was right—and I am sharing it now as a starting point for conversation. The line between instructing (or guiding) and restricting can be a fine one, and parenting leaves room for many mistakes. In our hearts, we all know that leading by example and keeping love and good intentions toward others as the motivation for all our actions will show our children what they really need to know.

Understanding Begins in the Home and Community

Cultural attitudes begin at home. Children naturally follow their parents' lead in their attitudes about others and about differing opinions and practices. A family culture of intolerance or exclusion will discourage diversity in all its forms, in both the parents' and their children's generations. But even if you never encountered differences in sexual orientation or gender identity beyond "normal" as a child, you still have the power to embrace differences now—to step back from the culture you were raised in and see new things in an accepting light.

As a parent, I loved my children unconditionally, encouraged individuality, and supported them. Some may say I was too lenient with my children. To them I say, you have no idea how strict I was; I really was. My children were raised in a Christian home, attending church and youth group. They were all honor students (most of the time), some were varsity athletes, others thespians. They participated in choir, took social dance, played football, tennis, and soccer. Rode motorcycles, grew up camping, hunting, fishing, hiking, cooking, baking, playing in band, and were surrounded by love, safety, and openness. They all volunteered throughout their growing-up years and would step in front of a bus to save any wayward animal in the street.

That all being said, I, like all parents, wanted the best and the easiest life for my children. I was scared when my gay son came out, but I educated myself and moved past my fear.

Several people I spoke with in the LGBTQ+ community expressed that it would be helpful to both the straight community and the LGBTQ+ community if gender roles and sexual identity were not thrust upon society from every direction. We pink-up the girls and blue-up the boys. We socially encourage girls to play with dolls, act ladylike, and become nurses. Conversely, we teach our boys to play any sport, act rough-and-tumble, and become surgeons. And we redirect our kids with little cues throughout their lives to show them the accepted, preferred way to appear, behave, and become.

"Janie, come set the table."

"Johnny, go carve the turkey."

"Elizabeth, you know you are not supposed to get your dress dirty!"

"Eric, look at you, all grown up and dirty from working just like your dad."

"Why don't you go play with your doll, Sara?"

"Samuel, where's your dump truck?"

Billboards and advertising are dominated by beautiful straight, cisgender couples. The only gay images advertisers show the public are beautiful "lipstick lesbians" and "macho gays" who could pass for straight. These attractive gay people are what is palatable and what the general public will accept, or so I am told. I am not even sure there is any serious advertising with transgender people; in fact, a transgender person told me that it would be helpful to transgender youth to see a transgender woman portrayed as something other than a prostitute on an episode of *Law & Order.*

Where sex education is still allowed and taught in schools, safe sex is discussed under the guise that everyone is straight with no discussion of safe gay sex or of transgender feelings of being in the wrong body. And in some religions, hellfire and damnation are promised to anyone other than straight, cisgender persons.

Of course there is fear—there is an onslaught of straight-cis advertising and a barrage of negative propaganda regarding gay and transgender people. They are bad. They are freaks, unnatural. They are not God's design. They do not deserve human or civil rights.

We can discriminate, hurt, berate, bully, overlook, underserve, and try to eliminate them from our otherwise hetero-cis world. And we are training our children to perpetuate this behavior. Why? Perhaps we are afraid they are going to take over our world and force us to "turn" gay or want a sex change. (Note: The term "sex change" is considered highly offensive and is not used in respectful conversation.) This is what I hear when I step back, ask people why they are so upset, and then listen to their words. People are naturally afraid of what is different and often lash out with aggression and violence. This has been seen throughout history: the Romans persecuted Christians, Americans enslaved Africans, Nazis exterminated the Jews, Hutu killed 70 percent of Tutsi in Rwanda, and today there are people in power who would like to "cleanse" society of gay and trans people.

These gay and transgender people are human beings just like you, just like me, and just like my children and yours. They are not asking for anything special. They do not require any different or special rights beyond decency and equality, and they are not "contagious"! You do not have to agree with their sexuality; they may not agree with yours. And you do not have to understand their need to transition genders, but you do need to understand they deserve the same chance to live their life and enjoy the same respect, decency, and support as anyone.

Hopes, Dreams, and Lives of LGBTQ+

PEOPLE IN THE LGBTQ+ COMMUNITY are your neighbors, your doctors, your child's teachers, your members of congress, your pastors, your coworkers, your friends, your children, your siblings, perhaps even your parents. And they want the exact same things as anyone one else.

When I asked gay and transgender people about the specifics of their lives, I received the kind of replies you might expect, some you might not.

- "I hate doing laundry and dishes," Chris said. "Andy hates laundry less. So our house usually has a full sink and pile of clean clothes on the couch."
- "We call ourselves 'comfortable gays.' We're not those 'fancy gays' you see on TV, we're the most heteronormative gay couple ever."
- "My intention in transitioning to live as Shannon wasn't to achieve a life-long dream of living as a woman. Transition

simply was a door to a more fulfilling life, free of the pain of hiding a huge part of me. I hope when people think of me they will see Shannon, a brave mother who decided to take control of her life."

- "I want to make lasting memories [with my son] and show him that he should never be afraid to be himself."
- "I want to find peace and happiness with a partner who understands me."
- "I want to see much more of the world and cultures that are dissimilar to my own."
- "I have always wanted kids."
- "I want to work with kids."
- "My hobbies are cross-stitching, reading, card making, and puppetry."
- "I dream of a world where all people are treated as the beloved children of God they are."
- "I love music, laughing, and spending time with friends and family."
- "I want to be able to make a living at a decent job that I enjoy and that provides benefits like healthcare and retirement."
- "I want to give my daughter the best start in the world that I possibly can, which includes teaching her to advocate for herself, help others, and find her niche."
- "I want financial security for my family and to be able to help others."
- "When I die I want to be surrounded by people who love me and who feel that I made their lives better for having been part of them."
- "I enjoy hiking, camping, and making furniture."
- "I try to be a good person and push my partner to be the best he can be."
- "Gay people bleed the same as straight people. We don't bleed glitter, and we don't ride unicorns and bake cookies all day."
- "I like watching people dance, and I love good music."

- "I am an artist. I like to draw, sketch, paint, and be creative."
- "I love to cook. I learned how to cook from my mother and grandmother."
- "I am a proud United States Navy veteran."
- "I want a decent place to live, enough food in the refrigerator, and to be able to pay my bills."
- "I try to be kind to everyone because you never know what someone else is going through."
- "The same things that make you cry make me cry."
- "I just want to be the best person I know how to be."
- "The only thing we can take with us when we die is how much we loved other people."

CHAPTER 8
Fear Within the LGBTQ+ Community

FEAR LIES ON BOTH SIDES of this subject—the fear of those who do not understand or empathize with the LGBTQ+ community and the fear of those who are LGBTQ+ living within a heteronormative, cisgender-dominant society.

For those in the LGBTQ+ community, the fear of being LGBTQ+ starts when they first recognize they are "different." Generally, this feeling begins in their youth. Without a supportive family or system to help them understand their difference, they often begin to act out, experiment with drugs or alcohol, become sexually promiscuous, and sometimes turn to self-harm as a coping mechanism or attempt suicide (as we've discussed already. But as a reminder, in the general population, the rate of attempted suicide is approximately 1.6 percent, compared to 41 percent of those identifying as transgender).

So why do those in this marginalized community have such fears and what are they afraid of?

Fear of Familial Rejection

IN AN EARLIER CHAPTER, WE explored the negative outcomes that can occur for LGBTQ+ people who come out to their family. This is a serious issue that warrants further discussion.

According to the Trevor Project, LGB youth who come from families that reject them are 8.4 times as likely to have attempted suicide as their LGB peers who reported no or low levels of family rejection.[44]

This alarming statistic explains in part why it's so hard for LGBTQ+ youth to come out to their family. Fear of negative reaction from one's family seems to rank as the number one biggest issue: "How is my family going to take this?" "Will they still love me?"

Mark, who came out many years ago, had such fears. As a priest, when he accepted his sexual orientation, he worried about his family—their reputation and his. He worried that people might think less of him for leaving the priesthood and coming out as gay. Mark struggled at length and sought in-depth counseling before approaching his family. Mark's family accepted him and has since accepted his partner without reservation. Mark's supportive and accepting family helped him become personally and entrepreneurially successful.

Chris T., however, turned to alcohol as a coping mechanism for his fear of lack of familial acceptance. He was fearful that his being gay would be a disappointment to his brother, whom he admired and whose support was essential to Chris, leading his brother to turn away from him. After years of alcohol abuse, he accepted the root issue surrounding his addiction and came out as gay. Chris reached the point that he needed to be true to himself regardless of the fallout, and he understood (as do most in this self-harming cycle) that for him to live, he would have to embrace his authentic self. Happily, Chris's brother and entire family accepted him for who he was—gay.

Rebekah inadvertently came out as lesbian to her family. She states that it was not her intention to actually come out, but she made a mistake with her "cover story" and her brother caught on.

She and Sue, who is now her wife, dated and then lived together for years. Rebekah and Sue lived in a two-bedroom place, indicating to the outside world that each of them lived in separate rooms. In reality, Rebekah and Sue had shared a room for years, and they'd even had a secret commitment ceremony. Rebekah laughs and states she and Sue referred to her room as the "straight room" for purposes of a cover story when her family would visit, so no one would be any the wiser. Then, one day during a visit to Rebekah and Sue's, Rebekah's sister-in-law had cold feet and asked for a pair of socks. Rebekah told her she had a pair she could borrow and directed her sister-in-law to what her sister-in-law knew as only Sue's room. Her sister-in-law and brother questioned why Rebekah's socks would be in Sue's closet. "I just lost it over something as stupid as wool socks," Rebekah said. She confided in her brother and sister-in-law, but her brother felt the need to tell their mother.

Rebekah cried in relief when she was able to be honest with her Evangelical missionary parents. Rebekah, who had always been told by her parents there was nothing she could do to stop them from loving her, could not grasp that this could include her being lesbian. She had heard mixed messages her entire life, "We will always love you," in conjunction with, "Gay is immoral, a sin, and prohibited [in their religion]." Rebekah was thirty-three years old when she came out, having lived in hiding regarding her sexuality since the age of twelve.

Unfortunately, some of Rebekah's fear of reprisal from her family was warranted. As the youngest of eight children, she was shunned, distanced, or completely cut off by several of her siblings. Her parents, however, accepted her and her relationship with Sue to the extent that her mother even encouraged them to have a child together. But Rebekah always felt a difference, to some degree, with her parents. She says that while they never stopped loving her, their relationship changed after she came out.

Rebekah shared that she had also feared how the children at her daughter's school would treat her daughter when they found out she had two mothers. Much to her relief, her fears were unfounded. Rebekah believes the children of the generation coming up are far more understanding, open, and tolerant. That is a feather in their parents' cap—an accomplishment they can be proud of.

Shannon, who is a transgender woman, stated, "I don't really have a family." She credited her parents for doing a wonderful job raising her and her brother, but she admitted that her personal turmoil over her gender confusion while growing up led to alcohol and substance abuse. "I think for my family, seeing me struggle with drugs and alcohol on top of having to digest the whole big change [of her transgender coming out], was just too much."

Once Shannon transitioned as a woman, her brother wanted nothing to do with her. This is made more difficult for Shannon, as she and her brother work across the hallway from each other in the same company. She states they have a professional relationship but nothing more.

"In the case of my mom, I see her, but we have a really distant relationship. I know she loves me, but everything has changed. I am in counseling now and seriously considering severing my relation-ship with my mother as it is toxic for me and completely unhealthy." Shannon's father reverts back to calling her his "son" when it is easier for him, especially around his friends, which is a bone of contention for Shannon that the she and her dad are working on.

Shannon knew that in order to save her own life she had to transition, regardless of the family cost. Shannon somewhat lost her parents, her only sibling, and her wife. Of note, Shannon and her ex-wife still co-parent their son and Shannon holds her ex-wife in the highest regard. "She just wasn't attracted to women," Shannon says of her.

Nichole states that she is creating her own new family. Since she has come out, there is a tremendous void due to the distance that appeared between her and her biological family, so she has surrounded herself with people who love and accept her as she is; she has found her "family of choice."

The fear of familial rejection is also seen in the foster system. Michelle Bass, a social worker directly involved with LGBTQ+ youth, wrote her thesis on "LGBTQ Youth Transitioning out of Foster Care."[45] In her research, she acknowledged a 2015 study by McCormick, Schmidt & Terrazas that noted LGBTQ youth living in non-accepting foster homes received different treatment than their non-LGBTQ foster youth counterparts. It was noted that the LGBTQ foster youth who were placed in non-accepting homes felt isolated and had difficulty building family and community connections.

Youth in these rejecting foster family situations were more restricted in the friends and love interests they were allowed to bring home, and they were also more closed off from communicating with their foster family and social workers. These youths experienced shame and had a tendency to internalize their feelings because they felt isolated.

Fear of Discrimination Abroad

UNIVERSALLY, MANY IN THE LGBTQ+ community fear traveling outside what they perceive to be their safe zone. Generally speaking, travel outside the United States is something everyone in the LGBTQ+ community considers seriously before doing. Same-sex parents must instruct their children on how to address them in foreign countries, as referring to both parents as Mom or as Dad could be dangerous. For some, if they can pass as straight, they may be less impeded with their travel.

Chris D. tries not to use the word fear because "we are all strong," he said. He instead prefers the word "anxiety." He said he has high anxiety regarding foreign travel and its possible dangers and, as such, has restricted himself from visiting certain areas of the world. These fears are legitimate, as there are several countries that criminalize gay and transgender people who face a punishment of life behind bars or, in some cases, death.

Shannon has encountered some of these same worries. Her work occasionally requires travel abroad, and she is fearful in certain places and so avoids them, in case she is recognized as transgender.

Fear of Hate Crime

THE DAY-TO-DAY LIFE THAT STRAIGHT, cisgender persons take for granted, such as holding hands while walking down the street with their partner, is something those in the LGBTQ+ community look at as a luxury.

Taylor, a young gay man, mentioned that he is uncomfortable with the eyes that are on him if he and his partner show any signs of affection in public. He gets anxious in anticipation for what he fears might be an attack or verbal abuse, so he chooses to forego public affection and do his best to go through society appearing to be straight. "People are so close-minded," he said. "I don't know why everyone is filled with so much hate. They are all preaching love, but that love is only for some."

"I was chased through a mall by a group of young boys," a transgender woman told me. "They were hurling slurs at me, and I was totally afraid for my safety."

A transgender man told me, "I was harassed by a group of church youth when I tried to use the bathroom at a city council meeting. I was at the meeting in support of an agenda item to add an anti-discrimination clause regarding LGBTQ+ persons to that city's ordinance."

As previously mentioned, bathrooms make many in the LGBTQ+ community uneasy because they are vulnerable and fearful for their safety. School locker rooms and gym settings also seem to make those in the LGBTQ+ community feel vulnerable and uncomfortable. This is especially true for youths.

George Godwyn is a cisgender social media influencer whose anti-establishment posts highlight social injustice and inequality. He has several outlets and speaks his mind, rather boldly, on subjects that appear to be close to his heart. I like his style, albeit shocking and vulgar at times. I read a post Godwyn wrote regarding the transgender bathroom situation. The individual who forwarded it to me (a transgender person) stated that while Godwyn is not transgender himself, it was still a very good, raw, and true depiction of what it is like to be transgender with all the hype surrounding the bathroom debate. It was certainly stomach-churning for me to read and I hope it makes the reader of this passage stop and think about today's bathroom issue for a transgender person. As is his usual in-your-face style of writing, his post was direct, succinct, and gut-wrenching. He started the post by saying, "For probably the first time, I am going to put a content warning on a post, because this post probably requires one. So, here's a CW for violence against trans people."

[And this writer is going to add a disclaimer for the remainder of this section. While Mr. Godwyn identified political conservatives by name, I choose to redact the names because I am not writing for any political agenda. I respect Mr. Godwyn's right to name names and would encourage the reader to check out his post directly for more specifics.]

Godwyn stated he had been curious about the transgender bathroom controversy and wondered why it was such a big deal to those on the conservative right. He posted a picture in a few large, conservative online groups of nearly half a million followers. This picture was of a transgender adult film actor, Buck Angel. The picture depicted Mr. Angel from the waist up, shirtless, buff, very muscular, with a shaved head and Fu Manchu mustache. The picture included the following question: "This person has a vagina. Which bathroom should they use?"

Godwyn's post received thousands of comments. Some were expected: "If they have a vagina then the women's room, if they have a penis, then the men's room." Godwyn wrote that he thought some people would respond by stating how potentially dangerous it would be if Mr. Angel were to use the ladies' room; that was not the case. The overwhelming number of similar responses were something Godwyn had never considered.

And here's where it gets disturbing. The commenters to the post had worked out a very simple solution to the problem of transgender people using public restrooms: They wanted transgender people to die. Godwyn wrote that these commenters were "quite explicit about it, very blunt. 'They should die.' That simple. That concise. 'They should die.'"

His post continued, "Let me be entirely clear about this—they knew what they were saying, they knew exactly what they wanted. They didn't want a trans man in the men's room and they didn't want a trans man in the women's room. They wanted the trans man to be dead."

Some of the commenters went so far as to give reasons why the transgender population should die, the preferred methods of how they should die, and some even admitted to fantasizing the deaths of transgender people. "Death or something similar was the most common answer," wrote Godwyn.

It was not only death that was threatened, it was torture, castration, and humiliation toward adults and children alike—any brutal, vicious insult or threat imaginable. Less vicious responses were "they should just stay home," meaning that if transgender people should be allowed to live, they should do it in private, away from others, behind closed doors.

Godwyn claimed to have spent much time over the years examining the people in these conservative social media groups and wrote that he didn't think anything could shock him, until he posted Mr. Angel's picture. The comments shocked him by the "sheer, stark, gut-level hatred, unencumbered by the slightest empathy. Loathing. Disgust. Raw hate." He added, "There is not one single issue that brings the evil out in [the conservative] supporters the way trans people do."

This post added a plea, asking the reader to think about all the

hate-filled comments and then consider a transgender man, present-
ing as male, being forced to use the ladies' room in a small town in
an ultra-conservative state. He then asked the reader to consider the
issue regarding teenagers—a transgender girl being forced to share
a bathroom with testosterone-hyped seventeen-year old boys, or a
transgender boy sharing the locker room with young girls.

These situations are not only unhealthy, they are dangerous
and may likely lead to disastrous outcomes. They may even cause
enough tension or strife to incite behavior that wouldn't have been
acted upon by otherwise nonviolent or nonaggressive people who
feel threatened. In uncomfortable situations, tempers flare, words
are said, people tend to lash out, and violence can ensue.

Godwyn summed up his post—and the feelings of this writer—
when he said, "Humiliation, violence, rape, suicide, and murder.
Death. Transgender rights are a matter of life and death, in a very
real, very palpable way. The definitions change and people die.
The rules change and people die. The laws change and people die.
Immediately."[46]

While the limelight is squarely on the transgender bathroom
issue, the bathroom is an issue for nearly all LGBTQ+ people.
Numerous assaults have occurred in bathrooms and locker rooms
where multiple people of all walks of life are forced to share their
private activities, such as using the toilet, showering, or changing
their clothes. These assaults, at a person's most vulnerable moments,
have created heightened awareness for those in the LGBTQ+ community that they are a target for these types of attacks. As such, they
have a greater fear of using communal bathrooms and locker rooms.

Those in the transgender community I spoke with all have a
near-phobia of open bathrooms and changing or locker rooms. And
most gay men have similar fears, choosing a single door bathroom

and using a closed, locking door to change behind. The lesbians I talked with about this subject for the most part did not have many concerns beyond what a person would normally have about using a toilet or changing in front of strangers.

I believe it goes without saying that violence of any kind can happen to anyone, but for those in the LGBTQ+ community, their statistics are exponentially higher than for those of us who identify as cisgender and straight.

We must stop the hate and the violence. We must stand up for and stand beside the people of the LGBTQ+ community.

CHAPTER 9

The Scourge of Hate Crimes

DISCRIMINATION COMES IN MANY FORMS, from simple harassment to criminal behavior—with hate crimes being the worst of the behaviors. Hate crimes are specifically directed toward an individual or group based on a prejudice of their race, religion, sexual orientation, or other bias.

In the United States, the legal term "hate crime" did not apply to acts of violence committed on the basis of gender identity, gender expression, or sexual orientation until 2009, when the Matthew Shepard and James Byrd, Jr. Hate Crimes Prevention Act was introduced. The Act expanded the hate-crime law to include crimes motivated by a victim's actual or perceived gender, sexual orientation, gender identity, or disability.

USA

New York City

In the early hours of June 28, 1969, New York City police raided the Stonewall Inn, a known gay club located on Christopher Street in Greenwich Village. This raid sparked six days of protests and violent clashes with law enforcement and served as a catalyst for the gay rights movement in the U.S. and around the world.[47]

The violence of the Stonewall Riots brought to light, in a dramatic way, the discrimination those in the LGBTQ+ community faced. It showed the world, perhaps for the first time, that there was a large population of people who were being brutally assaulted for their sexual orientation and gender identities.

This was a time when, in cities such as New York, there was a criminal statute that allowed police to arrest people wearing less than *three gender-appropriate articles of clothing*. During the Stonewall Riots, female officers took those suspected of cross-dressing into the bathroom to check their sex to see if they were violating the clothing statute.

At that time, it was also illegal to engage in "gay behavior" in public, such as holding hands, kissing, or dancing with someone of the same sex. An establishment could be shut down if it served alcohol to known or suspected LGBTQ+ individuals, as it was argued the mere gathering of gay people was "disorderly."[48]

Following Stonewall, and with today's instant media news, hate crimes against those in the LGBTQ+ community have become more and more visible.

Wyoming

Matthew Shepard was a twenty-one-year-old openly gay student at the University of Wyoming. On the evening of October 6, 1998, he was drinking a beer at a local bar when he met and began talking with two males of approximately the same age as Shepard. He later left with the two males for an unknown reason.

Through their own admission, these two individuals had planned to rob Shepard when they took him to a remote area in Laramie. Instead, however, an autopsy would reveal the two repeatedly struck Shepard in the head and face, between nineteen and twenty-one times, with the butt of a .357 pistol. They then bound Shepard's hands and tied him to a fence, taking his wallet and shoes.

Shepard was found approximately eighteen hours later by a cyclist who called for emergency help. Sheriff's deputy Reggie Fluty and emergency medical technicians responded. Fluty later reported that Shepard, who was only five feet, two inches tall and boyish in appearance, looked at first to be a child. His face was caked in blood except where tears had left tracks along his cheeks.[49]

Matthew Shepard would succumb to his injuries six days later. His attackers would both receive two consecutive life sentences for his murder.

Colorado

Fred Martinez was a Navajo youth slain at the age of sixteen for identifying as a two-spirit, a *nadleehi*, a male-bodied person with a feminine nature, i.e., transgender. In the Navajo culture, nadleehi is considered a special gift.

On the evening of Martinez's murder, an eighteen-year-old male approached Martinez, and the two ended up in a remote canyon area outside Cortez, Colorado, called The Pits. Martinez was found five days later, his stomach slashed and his skull crushed with a rock. The perpetrator, who apparently bragged to friends about "killing a fag," pled guilty to second-degree murder and is currently serving a forty-year sentence.

Texas

James Byrd, Jr. was a forty-nine-year-old black man who was picked up by three white men while walking home. The men severely beat Byrd and then chained him by his ankles with a logging chain to the back of a pickup truck. Byrd was dragged approximately three miles to his death. The autopsy report states that he was likely conscious until his head and arm were severed by a culvert. His torso was found a mile from his head and police found Byrd's remains in eighty-one different places. All three men were convicted of murder: one was sentenced to life in prison and the other two were sentenced to death.

Idaho

In April 2016, a twenty-three-year-old man posted a solicitation for sex on a website that was answered by forty-nine-year-old Steven Nelson. This post was apparently a ruse to rob Nelson. However, when Nelson met up with the man, he was attacked—kicked twenty to thirty times with steel-toed boots—while the man yelled anti-gay slurs at him.[50]

Nelson was then stripped of his clothes and robbed of his possession and his car. Nelson walked about a half-mile for help, naked and without shoes. He was taken to a local hospital where he was able to give a detailed description of the man who beat him. Nelson would die a few hours later from cardiac arrest.

Four men in total were accused and convicted in this heinous crime. One man, who described himself as the "salesman," helped orchestrate the ruse that would later lead to Nelson's death. Two other men also played a part in the death by hiding in the bushes during the attack, in case Nelson resisted and the other two required assistance.

The man who repeatedly kicked Nelson was charged and pled guilty to murder and a federal hate crime under the Matthew Shepard and James Byrd, Jr., Hate Crimes Prevention Act. The man known as the "salesman" was convicted of murder in the state court. The third and fourth men, the two in the bushes, both took plea deals admitting to aiding and abetting felony robbery. Their murder charges were dropped as a result of the pleas.

Nelson's death would again ignite the Add the Words movement (which would add the words "sexual orientation" and "gender identity" into the non-discrimination clause of the state's Human Rights Act) in Idaho, where Nelson lived and died. Steve Martin, the regional development organizer in Idaho for the Pride Foundation, stated following Nelson's death, "[T]he fact that we don't have legal protections statewide for gender identity and sexual orientation means that there's a perception that it's okay to discriminate."[51]

Bryan Lyda, program specialist with the Idaho Coalition Against Sexual and Domestic Violence[52] said, "When we push communities to the margins, we encourage people to live their lives in hiding to some degree, to seek relationships in ways that put them in dangerous situations."

At the time of writing this book, Add the Words has still not been added to Idaho's Human Rights Act and has not even made it to the floor of the legislature for a vote.

Australia

In the 1970s through the 1990s, there were dozens of what have been labeled as "Historic Gay-Hate Murders" in New South Wales, Australia. The majority of those eighty-eight victims of suspected anti-gay homicides were gay men, but several were transgender women. Many of these killings were brutal, including stabbings, strangulation, bludgeoning, shooting, sexual assaults, and frenzied attacks.[53]

There remain thirty unsolved cases of these so-called Gay-Hate Murders. Among those is the murder of twenty-seven-year-old American ex-pat, Scott Johnson.

Scott was a mathematician studying for his PhD in Sydney. He had a boyfriend of five years and his whole life in front of him. In 1988, Scott's naked body was found at the bottom of a cliff at North Head, New South Wales, his clothes neatly folded at the top of the cliff. Scott's death was ruled a suicide.

Scott's family was unwilling to accept this and fought for nearly three decades to be heard. It took two police investigations, three coronial inquests, letters from U.S. senators Elizabeth Warren and Edward Kennedy, a national television drama, and nearly one million dollars of Scott's brother's personal money to have Scott's cause of death ruled a gay-hate attack.[54]

Following these new investigations into the gay-hate murders, a report titled "Pursuit of Truth and Justice" was published by the leading LGBTI health organization, ACON. Following the report, Nicolas Parkhill, the CEO of ACON, stated of the killings: "It is important to note these events occurred in a time when homophobic and transphobic prejudice and hate permeated our society, thriving in many environments including government agencies, public institutions, courthouses, workplaces, communities, schools, and homes."

These events, unfortunately, do not seem to be isolated to only the 1970s to the 1990s that Mr. Parkhill referred to as the period of "homophobic and transphobic prejudice and hate." Similar incidents of horrendous and murderous behavior are still too common.

Chechen Republic, Russian Federation

As DISCUSSED PREVIOUSLY, SINCE 2017, anti-gay purges in the Chechen Republic have included the kidnapping, imprisonment and torture of at least 100 men suspected of being gay or transgender. These men are rounded up by local authorities, tortured for the names of others who identify as gay or transgender and sometimes released with the instruction to leave the country, or killed. The Russian leaders contend no such events have ever taken place.

El Salvador, Central America

SAME-SEX MARRIAGE IS NOT RECOGNIZED by law in El Salvador, and transgender people are not allowed to change to their gender on public documents.[55]

In 2016, twenty-five known members of the LGBTQ+ community were killed. In the first two months of 2017, seven known transgender people were murdered. One of those killed was Elizabeth Castillo, a transgender woman, who was kidnapped after attending the funeral of two transgender women. Her body, showing signs of torture, was dumped on the roadside.

"There is no doubt that the actions committed by these criminals are promoted by transphobia, machismo and the government's lack of interest (in urging) the police to conduct an exhaustive investigation to find those responsible and punish them for their acts," added Bryam Rodríguez of Generación de Hombres Trans de El Salvador, an organization based in the capital San Salvador.[56]

Latin America is the world's deadliest region for LGBTQ+ people, according to research group Transrespect Versus Transphobia Worldwide.

Elsewhere

THERE ARE APPROXIMATELY SEVENTY-FOUR COUNTRIES where being gay is a crime and there are approximately thirteen nations that have the death penalty for gay sex; four carry it out. Nations that have recently carried out executions are Iran and Saudi Arabia.

Nations that have no such law, but executions are carried out by militias and others are Iraq and Somalia.

Nations with such laws yet with no recent executions reported:

- Sudan
- Yemen
- Nigeria (Muslim northern part only)

Nations with such laws but with no executions reported:

- Afghanistan
- Mauritania
- Pakistan
- Qatar
- United Arab Emirates (some interpretations of law provide for the death penalty)
- Brunei Darussalam (it has not yet implemented a harsh new Sharia Penal Code Order which includes the death penalty for consensual same-sex sexual behavior).[57]

CHAPTER 10
Make an Effective Change: Lessons I Have Learned

"In the end we will not remember the words of our enemies, but the silence of our friends."
—Martin Luther King Jr.

I HAVE BEEN FORTUNATE TO meet some amazing people during the research for this project and am now friends with some. I would likely never have met these people were it not for this book. My eyes, my heart, and my mind have been opened to a group I have never interacted with before. My vocabulary has changed to be more sensitive, more inclusive, more understanding, and even more vulnerable.

I have learned that it is not okay to just "live and let live," as there are some groups of marginalized people who are not being allowed to just live. Why should I be okay with that? I am no longer satisfied to simply "take care of my own," and I will no longer stand in the shadows while other people stand up and do the fighting. I must become a warrior for those who are being persecuted, insulted, berated, and legislated out of existence. I have learned through my writing to stop living my life apathetically toward this and other marginalized communities and to be the one who stands up and speaks out for them and against hatred.

I have learned that while inequality, injustice, and inhumane treatment of this community of people are prevalent, it is not this community that has become the nuisance; it is those on the outside. The outsiders are the ones who are obnoxious, cruel, indignant, and loud. The outsiders are the group that rages with violence, terror, and hatred—not those being persecuted.

Those in the LGBTQ+ community merely want what the rest of us have; freedom to live their lives peacefully, make a living, enjoy their families and friends, contribute to society, and love their partners, spouses, and children. The LGBTQ+ community is not seeking special treatment or rights; they are seeking the freedoms already enshrined in the United States Constitution but which are being denied to them by bureaucrats, religious leaders, and hate groups. These same people, are now speaking maliciously about the many LGBTQ+ people who have served proudly in the military to defend their right to freedom of speech. The haters are trying to force these brave men and women out of their careers simply because of their sexual orientation or gender identity.

Religious leaders with LGBTQ+ people in their flock are sending them to slaughter when they come out. Rather than caring for them and protecting them (as prescribed in Matthew 25:40, "Truly I tell you, whatever you did for one of the least of these brothers, you did it to me"), they are turning their backs and telling them they are unworthy. Why are the religious leaders not protecting this group of people? Who are they to pass judgment?

People in authority (police and social workers) return LGBTQ+ children back to abusive and neglectful living situations rather than taking the children's concerns seriously and placing them in loving and nurturing environments.[58]

Powerful people are doing their best to send those in the LGBTQ+ community back into hiding, to criminalize their lives and in some cases attempt to eliminate them. I have seen how groups of people are blindly following these people in power. They are being dutiful and doing what they are told—that being it is okay to hate and discriminate against the lesbian, the gay, the transgender, the queer, the intersex, and the entire community. I suggest the people following the lead of the "powers that be" step back, get educated, and find their own thoughts and their own path regarding these human beings. What if it were your child who was gay or transgender? What if your son or daughter was questioning their gender or their sexual orientation?

It's easy to say you would disown them if you have never been faced with that decision or had to look in your child's eyes and say those words. We can all hide behind the pretense that it isn't about us or our children, and, therefore, we don't have to work for equality and do not have to care for the safety of LGBTQ+ people.

I have also learned that other groups of leaders, parents, school teachers and administrators, police, and social workers often do not seek to understand and educate themselves to the needs, desires, and fears of this community. Instead, they continue to believe that by using a strong arm, they can retrain, convert, scare, imprison, or as a last resort, simply cast out LGBTQ+ individuals from schools, homes, and society. Out of sight, out of mind.

But the most important thing I have learned is love and kindness; I have seen it and it is beautiful and worth noticing. I have watched the kind, gentle, fun, and loving spirits of several in this marginalized sector of people when they talk about what is happening to them and around them. They are angry, yes, but they are not violent. Either they know they will not win a fight by violence or they are simply the more intelligent and understand, better than those in charge, the ineffectiveness of aggression and violence. It is this marginalized community who are the calm, peace-desiring individuals, not the leaders, from what I have observed.

Learning from History

I DO NOT KNOW HOW to solve the problems at hand—the hatred, the segregation, the inequality, the violence—but this is a global issue that needs to be addressed and rectified. These issues are not new ones and are cyclical throughout history with other marginalized groups of people: the Jews, enslaved Africans, displaced tribal peoples, trafficked women, exploited children … the list is endless.

Women in America were not allowed to vote until 1920; Native Americans not until 1924; and African Americans until the mid-1960s. And while transgender persons are allowed to vote, they can only do so if their name and ID match their identity. These identity changes are neither easy nor cheap, and not everyone has the ability to navigate the system or the means to pay for these changes. The result is these people are less likely to have a voice in the people's government. Gay and lesbian people have no obvious barriers to being able to vote, other than the same risks they take every day that someone may choose to harass or attack them.

African Americans, Jewish people, Native Americans, and women have all had to fight to be desegregated, enjoy equality, and be counted as humans with rights. The LGBTQ+ community needs the same assistance to reach the same positive end goal: freedom to live their lives without fear of retribution for merely being alive.

Assistance for the LGBTQ+ community needs to come from cisgender, straight allies. Allies helped liberate those in concentration camps in Nazi Germany. Allies marched alongside people of color to end segregation. Allies advocated for Native Americans to become citizens of the land that was stolen from them decades prior. And men became allies of women in America to get voting rights. Our role as allies is to give whatever support is asked of us by those who are taking the fight forward for their cause.

Like the African Americans, Native Americans, people of the Jewish faith, and women, LGBTQ+ people are not going anywhere. They are not going to be erased, eradicated, or wished into nonexistence, even if laws and regulations do not support them. Have we not learned anything from our ancestors?

Starting a Positive Conversation

A POSITIVE CONVERSATION NEEDS TO be had, and it can start at home. Encourage inclusion and ban hatred from your table talk, walk away from people who are bigots and shamers, and stop supporting bad behavior through your silence.

Support your family. Love your children for who they are and remember, regardless of their age, they are still your children. Teach them to practice acceptance and understanding instead of bias and judgment.

Keep in mind that when people come out as LGBTQ+, they still need their parents, their friends, and their respectful coworkers. These people are *human beings*. Don't throw them away because you don't understand who they are or what they are going through. They are struggling to live a life that is true to who they are—something we all strive to do.

I am not gay, so I cannot fully understand what it is to be gay, even after raising a gay son and watching him strive to live his authentic life. But I have looked in his eyes and know I will never stop loving him. I know he has dreams for his future and plans to use his degree in biology to go into vaccinology and cancer research. I know he is a foodie who enjoys hiking and hanging out with his friends. He has used his engaging personality as a means to support himself as a waiter through college, and I hear his voice singing in my head anytime an ABBA song comes on the radio. He is an American citizen in the pursuit of happiness, just as every other citizen of this country. I will not stand by while someone speaks disparagingly about him or others in the LGBTQ+ community, and I will stand up for him and for all people to be treated equally and with kindness. It is that simple.

For suggestions on starting points, please see the section titled "Communication Tools and Starting Points."

Appeals from the LGBTQ+ Community

CHRIS D., A GAY MAN whose family never accepted him, said, "Hurt and abandonment is a big part of our community; I think everyone in this community identifies with that. And to parents: 'Don't be assholes!' Love and accept your kids, make sure they know they are loved. Especially to the parents who are struggling with the in-your-face gay phase, it is very hard. Be patient; let them find who they are."

Chris D. wants people to know the LGBTQ+ community has more in common with the rest of society than they have differences—they are just people, after all. He said to me with his boyish charm, "Now that you know me personally, it's hard to hate me, isn't it?"

He also said, "I think a lot of parents feel they have done something wrong because their child is gay. They haven't, it's just who they [the children] are."

Shannon, a transgender woman who frankly and honestly told me her story and shared the most serious issues she faces daily, made several statements about what would have helped her feel less isolated, less threatened, and what she thinks would make effective change:

- "I don't know what would have made it [questioning my gender and transitioning] better for me, I think seeing yourself in the media and represented is powerful. Having positive role models out there saying, 'Here's someone who's trans and they are doing okay at life.' That has to help."
- "I look at the families that do have trans kids and do support them—all they have to do is love their kid and show up. They don't have to come programmed. As parents, we don't have to know everything about every single situation our child is going to encounter."

- "The parents who show up and are honest and say, 'My child feels this way and I'm scared and I don't know what to do.' That first step … those families who are going to support their kids—their kids are going to be okay. It's really just about showing up, being vulnerable."
- "And when you see someone like me walking down the street, just treat me like everyone else. I think that helps kids who are closeted to know, 'Hey, my parents don't see this as a big deal, and perhaps if I came out, they wouldn't see it as a big deal.'"

William Mathis, who feels responsible in part for his daughter Patti's suicide because of his initial reactions to her coming out, said this: "We need to realize we need to accept our children if they are gay and love them and let them know we are there to support them and treat them right."

Drew, who identifies as an asexual non-binary person, also focused on family as the place to start: "I know parents who just won't deal with it—not that they can't, they just won't. They don't want to hear about it. They are hurting themselves and their children. If my parents are getting this at their age [eighties], then anyone can!"

Rebekah is a married lesbian who, with her wife, is raising a daughter in an ultra-conservative state, has this message for parents of LGBTQ+ youth: "You just have to be open. Don't put them in a box. Whatever's going to happen is going to happen. Try to keep them from making big mistakes—don't get pregnant, don't quit school, don't kill yourself."

Chera Kelsey, a social worker whose work is intertwined with LGBTQ+ youth and who has a young family member who recently came out lesbian, said this: "Try to be available. People need to be able to have the space to feel heard. When your family rejects you or there is distance or avoidance, and when you don't have the ability to connect spiritually or when you are in the faith system and then the consequence of living authentically is lost, I think that is a whole other layer that complicates the depression and suicide attempts."

Carolyn Blackhurst, an LGBTQ+ advocate who is active in her church and community, said, "[A] nondiscrimination ordinance is a tangible way to provide protection and to send a message to our youth, to businesses, and to our nation, that in this great city you are welcome and you matter."

"I would rather have a gay son than a dead son," said Kerri, the mother of a gay young man.

Chris T., a gay man who lived in hiding for years because he feared family rejection, said, "The only thing we can take with us is how we loved other people for who they are."

When I asked my own son, Hunter, if he had any advice to help others better understand the coming out of a gay person, he said, "Keep in mind that when young men and women come out in their teens, their brains are still developing. That this is a heightened time of depression, regardless of sexual or gender identity. There is anxiety and mania to think about and there are more generally unfounded emotions at this age. Be sensitive toward your children. Encourage them to be who they are, and do not put them in a box. Your acceptance now can be the turning point for their survival later."

And in the easy words of Taylor, who is an extremely accomplished artist, his advice is that not everyone will make a public statement regarding their sexuality, and that is okay. "You didn't announce you were heterosexual, why should I come out as gay?"

Nichole, a young lesbian still trying to grapple with the fallout of her family since her coming out said, "Family means everything to me. I just hope that before I die, or one of my aunts or uncles dies, that we can all come back together as a family."

George Godwyn, who wrote the gut-wrenching article about the transgender public restroom issue referred to previously, said, "There are no people so vulnerable, so marginalized, and there should be no doubt about this. If we don't stop this, people are going to die, killed for something they can't change, for who they are in the deepest part of themselves. Not somewhere down the road, not in five years, but now. They're going to start dying now."

While it is easy to point out the obvious differences between straight, cisgender people and LGBTQ+—who they are or are not attracted to, and whether they feel comfortable in the body they were born in—there are far more similarities between these groups of people than differences. And the similarities go much deeper. All people have a need to fit in, to be heard, to be loved. Every human deserves fair and equal treatment.

Each of us desires the love and respect of our families, friends, and colleagues. We all want to live in peace and have a safe environment. We all share the same essential feelings, hopes, and desires. There is not one group of people who has cornered the market on suffering. There is no group, race, or person who is above the other when it comes to the inescapable facts of life and death from the chances of getting cancer to the vulnerability to the common cold. Every person must urinate, defecate and, at times, vomit. We all bleed. Every one of us was created in the same way in the uterus. True, no two of us are alike, but why do we feel a small portion of these precious children should be considered unworthy?

There is an argument for every position and there will always be someone unwilling to agree to disagree. And, there will always be those who feel that their beliefs are the only correct ones. But we are hurting each other by being obstinate and oppressive. What gives one group the idea they are better than others and have the license to behave poorly?

This book will not solve the world's problems and will not curb the hate and animosity that has existed between different groups of people since the beginning of time, but it is my hope that it will, at least, start some positive conversations between the two groups. And just maybe, it may bring together a family otherwise divided by sexual orientation or gender identity.

"I believe that telling our stories, first to ourselves and then to one another and the world, is a revolutionary act. It is an act that can be met with hostility, exclusion, and violence. It can also lead to love, understanding, transcendence, and community."

— **Janet Mock** in *Redefining Realness: My Path to Womanhood, Identity, Love & So Much More*

ACKNOWLEDGMENTS

IT GOES WITHOUT SAYING IF it were not for the willingness by those I spoke with in the LGBTQ+ community to be open, raw, and vulnerable with me, this book would not have become a reality. The stories told, tears shed, and emotions shared will never be forgotten, and some will always haunt me.

To say I learned a lot through this writing is as big an understatement as I can imagine. In full transparency, I was initially only going to write about gay and lesbian people. Having a gay child made this easy for me to wrap my head around. But, my son, Hunter, whom I reference throughout this book, said to me, "Mom, you absolutely must write about the transgender population. They're the most overlooked and marginalized of all of us; they are the ones who need a voice."

Thank you, Hunter, for being the encouragement, the kick in the behind, and the support I needed when I was discouraged and afraid to write difficult, unpopular words. I love you to the moon and back.

A big thank you to Mascot Books and all those involved in this project for standing with me. Their names, as with mine, will forever be attached to a controversial subject matter at a time when it wasn't mainstream popular to stand up for those in the LGBTQ+ community. (I hope people years from now read that line and laugh at its absurdity.) In particular, thank you, Kate, Nina, Chris, and Lorna.

And to the many others who didn't abandon me during this project, Carolyn for reading everything I ever write and still loving me (thanks, Ethel, ~Lucy), Kowboy and Linnea, Adam and Hanna—I love you. My pastor friends, Larry and Marci, for your Biblical insight; Michelle, for always having my "legal" back; and the many others who continue to support me.

To my biggest supporter, my husband, Jody. Thank you for supporting me through the social media haters, for never fading when the going gets tough, and for always being on my side.

RESOURCES
LGBTQ+ Language

LANGUAGE CHANGES CONSTANTLY, BUT THE terminology in the LGBTQ+ lexicon changes even more frequently as society becomes more attuned to the power that words have to discriminate and oppress. Below is a list of the most commonly used terms, but for the most comprehensive, up-to-date glossary, visit www.glaad.org/reference/lgbtq.

Ally – An individual who speaks out and stands up for a person or group that is targeted and discriminated against. An ally works to end oppression by supporting and advocating for people who are stigmatized, discriminated against, or treated unfairly.

Asexual – Without sexual feeling or association. An asexual person may have sexual attraction, but the attraction does not need to be realized in any sexual manner.

Binary – Both masculine and feminine.

Bisexual – Someone who is sexually attracted to both males and females.

Cisgender – A person whose gender identity correlates with their sex at birth. *Opposite of transgender.* Can be referred to as "Not transgender."

Cross-Dresser – A person who dresses to give the appearance of the opposite gender, be it with the use of clothing, makeup, or accessories socially ascribed to that specific gender. **NOTE: A transgender woman (a man who gender identifies female) is neither a drag queen nor a cross-dresser.**

Dead Name – A person's former, given name, usually the name given at birth and no longer used. It is a disrespect to refer to someone by their dead name.

Drag Queen – Generally known as a man who dresses in women's clothing and makeup and uses a caricatured feminine persona for entertainment purposes.

Gay – A male who is sexually attracted to other men. Also used to refer to anyone (male and female) whose sexual orientation is same-sex.

Gender Confirmation Surgery (GCS) – The process of surgically altering a person's sex assigned at birth to align with their gender identity. **DO NOT use the term "Sex Change Operation."** Also called **Sex Reassignment Surgery (SRS).**

Gender Dysphoria – The modern-day term (coined 2013) for the condition of a mismatch of physical sex and gender identity. The term was defined in the *Fifth Edition of the American Psychiatric Association Diagnosis and Statistical Manual of Mental Disorders* (DSM-V). Both psychiatric and medical authorities recommend individualized medical treatment through hormones and/or surgeries to treat gender dysphoria. Some advocates believe the inclusion of Gender Dysphoria in the DSM is necessary in order to advocate for health insurance that covers the medically necessary treatment recommended for transgender people. (*GLADD Media Reference Guide – Transgender GLADD*, https://www.glaad.org/reference/transgender.)

Gender Expression – External, outward expression of gender expressed through a person's name, pronouns, clothing, haircut, behavior, voice, and/or body characteristics. These cues are identified as masculine or feminine. Typically, transgender people seek to align their gender expression to their gender identity rather than the sex they were assigned at birth.

Gender Identity – A person's sense of their gender. Transgender persons have a sense that their identity does not match the sex they were assigned at birth (gender dysphoria).

Gender Non-Conforming (GNC) – Indicative of a person whose behavior or appearance does not conform to cultural or social expectations for that gender. **NOTE: Gender Non-Conforming does not indicate a person as transgender or transsexual.**

Gender Shaming – Associated with gender roles and the stereotypical behavior which, if women or men fail to abide by they are called names that refer to them as socially and/or gender inadequate.

Heteronormative and Gendernormative – Denoting or relating to the worldviews that straight and cisgender are the norm.

Intersex – A person for whom there is a discrepancy between the external genitals and the internal genitals (the testes and ovaries). A general term used in which a person is born with a reproductive or sexual anatomy that doesn't fit the typical definitions of female or male.

LGBTQIA+ (LGBTQ+) – Acronym for Lesbian, Gay, Bisexual, Transgender, Queer (or Questioning), Intersex, and Asexual (or sometimes Ally). The "+" symbol indicates "all the rest" in that community. There are as many as ninety or so different categorizations that have been identified regarding a person's sexual orientation and gender identity, therefore, the most-used acronym is "LGBT" or "LGBTQ."

Lesbian – A female who is sexually attracted to other females. A gay woman.

Mx (pronounced mux or mix) – This is a title (to replace Ms., Mrs., Mr.) used by those who do not identify as a specific gender or prefer not to be identified as a gender.

Non-Binary (or genderqueer) – Terms used by people who experience their gender identity and/or gender expression as falling outside the categories of man and woman. They may define their gender as falling somewhere in between man and woman or they may define it as wholly different from these terms. **NOTE: this is not synonymous with transgender or transsexual.**

Pansexual – Not limited in choice as to sex, gender, or gender identity.

Pass – The ability for a gay or transgender person to *pass* through society without being recognized as gay or transgender.

Sexual Orientation – Describes a person's enduring physical, romantic, and/or emotional attraction to another person. Gender identity and sexual orientation are not the same. E.g., a person who transitions from male to female and is attracted solely to men would typically identify as a straight woman.

Sex Reassignment Surgery (SRS) – See **Gender Confirmation Surgery (GCS)**.

Trans – An abbreviation for transgender and/or transsexual.

Transgender – A person whose gender identity and gender expression differ from the sex they were assigned at birth. Not all transgender persons will alter their body to fit their gender identity. A transgender person does not have to alter their body to be transgender.

Transition (Transitioning) – The process of altering one's born sex to align with one's gender expression. A person can be considered transitioning by openly dressing and behaving in the manner of another gender, changing their name (either legally or socially) and/or by using hormones or surgery to transition to the opposite gender. **AVOID the term "Sex Change."**

Transsexual – A term used when a person has altered their body to fit their gender identity by means of hormones or surgery. It is important to use the term requested by the person, either transsexual or transgender, because they are different terms.

Transvestite – A person who derives pleasure from wearing clothes of the opposite gender. This does not mean the person is transgender or transsexual.

COMMUNICATION TOOLS AND STARTING POINTS

Be available. It is especially important for families to be available to their children when they come out. It is okay to not know what to say; in fact, saying that you don't know what to say is acceptable to say! Remember, the person who is coming out to you has generally had a lifetime to accept their coming out, while you have just learned of it. Be patient with yourself but be available.

Don't be in the closet about your support. It can be equally damaging to support your LGBTQ+ family member or friend in private but not stand up for them in public. Not everyone will want to march in a parade (I attended my first PRIDE event in 2019), but at least support the LGBTQ+ community to your peers. It's easily done, whenever someone starts a negative conversation, to simply remind them that you have a family member or friend within that community. Introduce your loved one's significant other honestly, e.g., "This is my daughter's partner" or "Their preferred pronouns are 'he' and 'his.'"

Require respect from your family. Tell your family clearly that unless they respect your LGBTQ+ family member or friend, you will not be attending family social events. Be prepared to not get invited, too. It may be hurtful, but your LGBTQ+ loved one will know where they stand with you and they will know you support them.

Encourage education. Lack of understanding begets fear, which in turn can beget violence. There are plenty of websites, videos, and other sources of information available to help those outside the LGBTQ+ community have a better understanding about anti-gay and anti-trans issues.

Confront anti-gay and anti-trans behavior. Let people in your life know it is not okay to "joke" about gays or transgender people. Every time you stand up against anti-LGBTQ+ behaviors, you encourage better behavior.

Reach out to your congressperson. Sign the petitions, write to your legislators, get active behind the scenes if being at the parades is not for you. Be the voice of the allies for the LGBTQ+ community: they need it.

Always use the person's preferred name. Whether or not a person has legally changed their name, if they prefer to use a certain name it should be used. It is disrespectful to continue to use a person's "dead" name.

Use preferred pronouns. It is important to identify people using their preferred pronouns, i.e., he/him, she/her, they/them (the plural pronoun form is increasingly used in the singular form for gender neutral purposes). It may sound odd using "they" or "them" as a singular, but it is appropriate to people whose gender identity is asexual or fluid. It is also appropriate to use "they" and "their" in a singular context if you are unsure how to refer to the person.

It's okay to ask how to refer to someone. If you are unsure how to address someone or which pronouns to use simply say, "My name is Lynda, and my preferred are she and her." The appropriate response in return will be the person giving you their name and preferred pronouns.

Use inclusive language. When referring to people in general, try using words like "partner." instead of "boyfriend/girlfriend" or "husband/wife," and avoid gendered pronouns, using "they" and "their" instead of "he/she."

Stay away from slang words unless specifically given permission. While those in the LGBTQ+ community may call themselves names such as "dyke," "fag," "queer," or "tranny," it is NOT okay for you to do it. And if you feel you must try these words out with your friend or family member, get their permission. These words are derogatory and completely inappropriate otherwise. "Homosexual" can also be seen in a negative light, so use it cautiously. It is best to stick with the more accepted gay, lesbian, bisexual, transgender, and questioning.

Use inclusive, affirmative, anti-discrimination signs in the workplace and in businesses. Post a sign that states, "We provide equality of services and care to everyone, regardless of age, disability, gender, gender identity, race, religion or belief, or sexual orientation." An easy way is to simply post: "EVERYONE welcome."

Additionally, post a "safe zone," "safe space" sign or a PRIDE rainbow symbol or pink and blue transgender triangle has become a quick way for those in the LGBTQ+ community to recognize they are safe to be themselves in your presence.

Safe space. Provide a welcoming, supportive, and safe environment for lesbian, gay, bisexual, and transgender people.

Don't assume straight/cisgender (and don't assume just because someone supports LGBTQ+ means they are LGBTQ+). Just because a person appears a certain way does not mean they are. Period.

Learn the facts[59].

- This is not "just a phase." Embrace—don't dismiss—someone's evolving sense of self.
- There is no "cure." It is not something that needs to be fixed.
- Don't look for blame: neither you nor your child did anything wrong. Instead, celebrate your children and all that they are.

Stay involved in your child's school[60].

- Advocate for a gay-straight alliance (GSA), which has been shown to make schools safer and boost academic performance among LGBTQ students.
- Maintain frequent contact with teachers. That way, you'll know when issues arise.
- Push for more inclusive sex education. Very few states allow schools to provide LGBTQ students with the information they need to be safe and healthy. Be aware of these knowledge gaps so that you can fill them yourself.
- Above all, don't hesitate to speak up. It's okay to go to the teacher, the administrator, the principal or the school board with concerns.

Look out for signs of bullying[61].

Bullying is a problem for many students, but LGBTQ youth

in particular are often targeted for being different. If you see the following signs, reach out to a teacher, guidance counselor, or school administrator:

- Behavior change (e.g., your outgoing, sociable child is now withdrawn)
- Discipline or behavioral problems in school
- Declining grades
- Unexplained absences
- Sudden shifts in who's a friend and who's not
- Engagement in risky behavior (e.g., drug use, new sexual partner) that is out of character for your child

Seek counseling and support. Having a family member come out as LGBTQ+ can be overwhelming, frustrating, and complicated. You are not alone in these feelings. Seek counseling that specializes in families going through this transition and look for support groups in your community and online.

Stay involved in your LGBTQ+ child's social and dating circles. Whether LGBTQ+ or not, it is important for parents to stay involved with their child's friends and love interests. Know who these people are, find out about their background, and meet their parents. Become involved and engaged. Encourage healthy relationships based on mutual respect, trust, and love.

Keep up on your LGBTQ+ child's social media. If an LGBTQ+ child is feeling misunderstood, unaccepted, or unloved, they will turn to those they feel will better understand and accept them. The internet is loaded with predators that look for vulnerable youth. Stay involved.

COMMUNITY SUPPORT

Suicide Prevention

TRANSGENDER SUICIDE HOTLINE IN THE U.S.: 877-565-8860, translifeline.org

LGBTQ suicide and crisis hotline/helpline, The Trevor Project, 866-488-7386, thetrevorproject.org/get-help-now

Resources below are from the Center for Disease Control: "Links to non-federal organizations found at this site are provided solely as a service to our users. These links do not constitute an endorsement of these organizations or their programs by CDC or the Federal Government, and none should be inferred. CDC is not responsible for the content of the individual organization Web pages found at these links."

Resources for LGBTQ+ Youth and Friends/Supporters

- healthychildren.org: *Gay, Lesbian, and Bisexual Teens: Facts for Teens and Their Parents*
- glsen.org: *Gay, Lesbian & Straight Education Network (GLSEN): Student Action*
  Advice for students who want to make change in their school and community.
- gsanetwork.org: *Genders & Sexualities Alliance Network*
  A GSA club is a student-run club in a high school or middle school that brings together LGBTQI+ and straight students to support each other.
- itgetsbetter.org: *It Gets Better Project*
  The It Gets Better Project reminds teenagers in the LGBT community that they are not alone and it will get better.
- qcardproject.com: *Q Card Project*
  The Q Card is a simple and easy-to-use communication tool designed to empower LGBTQ youth to become actively engaged in their health and to support the people who provide their care.
- StopBullying.gov: *Information for LGBT Youth*
  Lesbian, gay, bisexual, or transgender (LGBT) youth and those perceived as LGBT are at an increased risk of being bullied. There are important and unique considerations for strategies to prevent and address bullying of LGBT youth.
- thetrevorproject.org: *The Trevor Project: Crisis Intervention and Suicide Prevention*
  The Trevor Project is a national organization providing crisis intervention and suicide prevention services to lesbian, gay, bisexual, transgender, and questioning (LGBTQ) young people, ages 13 to 24.

Resources for Educators and School Administrators

BECAUSE SOME LGBTQ+ YOUTH ARE more likely than their straight peers to experience bullying or other aggression in school, it is important that educators, counselors, and school administrators have access to resources and support to create a safe, healthy learning environment for all students.

- *Advocates for Youth (AFY): LGBTQ Resources for Professionals*: Advocatesforyouth.org. Includes lesson plans, tips and strategies, background information, and additional resources to help youth-serving professionals create safe space for young people of all sexual orientations and gender identities.
- American Psychological Association (APA) Resources
- *Healthy Lesbian, Gay and Bisexual Students Project*: apa.org/pi/lgbt/programs/hlgbsp/index.aspx. The Safe and Supportive Schools Project promotes safe and supportive environments to prevent HIV and other sexually transmitted infections among adolescents.
- *Just the Facts: A Primer for Principals, Educators, and School Personnel*: apa.org/pi/lgbt/resources/just-the-facts.aspx. Just the Facts provides information and resources for principals, educators and school personnel who confront sensitive issues involving gay, lesbian and bisexual students.
- *Understanding Sexual Orientation and Gender Identity*: apa.org/helpcenter/sexual-orientation.aspx. Accurate information for those who want to better understand sexual orientation.
- *Bullied: A Student, a School and a Case That Made History: Teaching materials for educators*: tolerance.org/classroom-resources/film-kits/bullied-a-student-a-school-and-a-case-that-made-history. "Bullied" is designed to help administrators,

teachers and counselors create a safer school environment for all students, not just those who are gay and lesbian.

- *Gay, Lesbian & Straight Education Network (GLSEN): Educator Resources*: glsen.org/educate/resources/guides. Educator guides and lessons to support your curriculum and practices.
- *Genders and Sexualities Alliance (GSA) Network: Transforming Schools*: glsen.org/participate/student-action/gsa. GSA clubs can make schools safer and more welcoming for LGBTQ youth.
- *HIV/AIDS and Young Men Who Have Sex with Men*: cdc.gov/healthyyouth/sexualbehaviors/pdf/hiv_factsheet_ymsm.pdf. Learn more about how HIV disproportionately affects young men who have sex with men.
- *National Alliance to End Homelessness: Serving LGBT Homeless Youth*: b.3cdn.net/naeh/9edec5bddd88cea03d_yum6be7c4.pdf. To end LGBT youth homelessness, youth and young adults need stable housing, supportive connections to caring adults, and access to mainstream services that will place them on a path to long-term success.
- *National Education Association: Bullying Prevention Resources*: nea.org/home/51929.htm. Educators know that that every student deserves a safe, welcoming, affirming learning environment. In fact, research shows that learning is stunted when the need to feel safe and respected is not met.
- *Questions and Answers: LGBTQ Youth Issues*: pflag.org/sites/default/files/Be%20Yourself.pdf. Questions and answers on sexual orientation, gender identity, and risks or challenges some LGBTQ youth may experience.
- *StopBullying.gov: Information for Educators and Other School Professionals*: stopbullying.gov. Schools are a place where bullying can happen. Helping to establish a supportive and safe school climate where all students are accepted and knowing how to respond when bullying happens are key to making sure all students are able to learn and grow.

- *The Trevor Project: Education and Resources for Adults*:
  thetrevorproject.org/resources/preventing-suicide/how-can-
  you-help/trevor-care-training/broken-adult-education-faq/#
  sm.00000fo8y9xk9bdhwuj544oxeyg1p. The Trevor Project's
  "Trainings for Professionals" include in-person Ally and CARE
  trainings designed for adults who work with youth. These
  trainings help counselors, educators, administrators, school
  nurses, and social workers discuss LGBTQ-competent suicide
  prevention.

Resources for Parents, Guardians, and Family Members

SOME LGBTQ+ YOUTH ARE MORE likely than their straight peers to experience negative health and life outcomes, so it is critical for the parents, guardians, and other family members to have access to the resources they need to ensure their LGBTQ+ children are protected and supported.

- *Advocates for Youth (AFY): Our bodies. Our lives. Our Movement*:
  advocatesforyouth.org. LGBTQ youth need respect, support,
  and someone to listen to them.
- *Electronic Aggression*: youth.gov/youth-topics/teen-dating-
  violence/electronic. How increased access to technology has
  benefits but also increases the risk of abuse.
- *The Family Acceptance Project*: familyproject.sfsu.edu. The
  Family Acceptance Project is a research, intervention,

education, and policy initiative that works to prevent health and mental health risks for LGBT children and youth.

- *Gay, Lesbian, and Bisexual Teens: Information for Teens and Their Parents*: patiented.solutions.aap.org/handout. aspx?gbosid=156690. Finding out your son or daughter is gay, lesbian, or bisexual can be difficult. "A message to parents" can help you learn more about how to engage with your child on this topic.

- *A Practitioner's Resource Guide: Helping Families to Support Their LGBT Children*: store.samhsa.gov/product/A-Practitioner-s-Resource-Guide-Helping-Families-to-Support-Their-LGBT-Children/PEP14-LGBTKIDS. This resource guide was developed to help practitioners who work in a wide range of settings to understand the critical role of family acceptance and rejection in contributing to the health and well-being of adolescents who identify as LGBT.

- *KidsHealth.org: Sexual Attraction and Orientation*: kidshealth. org/en/teens/sexual-orientation.html. Information for parents on how youth experience sexual attraction and orientation, as well as how you as a parent or guardian may feel about and deal with youth on this topic.

- *Parents, Families, Friends, and Allies of Lesbians and Gays (PFLAG)*: pflag.org. Information about PFLAG's confidential peer support and education in communities.

- *Parents' Influence on the Health of Lesbian, Gay, and Bisexual Teens: What Parents and Families Should Know*: cdc.gov/ healthyyouth/protective/pdf/parents_influence_lgb.pdf. Information on how parents can promote positive health outcomes for their LGB teen.

- *StopBullying.gov: What you can do, Information for Parents, Educators and Community*: stopbullying.gov/what-you-can-do/index.html. Parents play a key role in preventing and responding to bullying. If you know or suspect that your child is involved in bullying, here are several resources that may help.

- *Supportive Families, Healthy Children: Helping Families with Lesbian, Gay, Bisexual and Transgender Children*: cchealth.org/ topics/lgbtq/pdf/supportive_families.pdf. A family model to increase family support, decrease risk, and promote the well-being of LGBT children and youth.
- *Understanding Sexual Orientation and Gender Identity*: plannedparenthood.org/learn/sexual-orientation-gender. Accurate information for those who want to better understand sexual orientation.

REFERENCES

1   Casey Wong, "Homosexuality in Nazi Germany," *Wiener Library Blog,* October 31, 2017, https://wienerlibrary.co.uk/Blog?item=272&returnoffset=.

2   Masha Gessen, "The Year Russian L.G.B.T. Persecution Defied Belief," *The New Yorker,* December 29, 2017, https://www.newyorker.com/culture/2017-in-review/the-year-russian-lgbt-persecution-defied-belief.

3   Thomas Burrows, "Chechnya opens world's first concentration camp for homosexuals since Hitler's in the 1930s where campaigners say gay men are being tortured with electric schocks and beaten to death," *Mailonline,* April 10, 2017, https://www.dailymail.co.uk/news/article-4397118/Chechnya-opens-concentration-camp-homosexuals.html.

4   Matt Baum, "Chechnya's Gay Purge is Escalating. The US Has Done Almost Nothing to Help," *Them,* January 25, 2019, https://www.them.us/story/chechnya-gay-purge-2019.

5   Sam Manzella, "FBI: Anti-LGBT Hate Crimes are on the Rise—Especially against Trans Americans," *Logo NewNowNext,* November 14, 2017, http://www.newnownext.com/fbi-hate-crimes-lgbt/11/2017/.

6   Lamar Dawson, "The LGBT Murder Rate Skyrocketed Nearly 90% Last Year," *Logo NewNowNext,* April 19, 2018, http://www.newnownext.com/lgbt-gay-hate-crime-murder-homicide/04/2018/.

7   Brian S. Barnett, Ariana E. Nesbit and Renee M. Sorrentino, "The Transgender Bathroom Debate at the Intersection of Politics, Law, Ethics, and Science," *Journal of the American Academy of Psychiatry and the Law,* June 2018, 46(2) 232-241, http://jaapl.org/content/46/2/232/tab-article-info.

8   Clara Moskowitz, "5 Myths about Gay People Debunked," Live Science, March 25, 2011, https://www.livescience.com/13409-myths-gay-people-debunked-sexual-orientation.html.

9   The Bronfenbrenner Center for Translational Research, "Checking up on the Science of Homosexuality," May 12, 2016, https://www.psychologytoday.com/us/blog/evidence-based-living/201605/checking-the-science-homosexuality.

10   Shankar Vedantam, "The Scarcity Trap: Why we keep digging when we're stuck in a hole," *Hidden Brain*, March 20, 2017, https://www.npr.org/2017/03/20/520587241/the-scarcity-trap-why-we-keep-digging-when-were-stuck-in-a-hole.

11   Jaimie Seaton, "Homeless rates for LGBT teens are alarming, but parents can make a difference," *Washington Post,* March 29, 2017, https://www.washingtonpost.com/news/parenting/wp2017/03/29/homeless-rates-for-lgbt-teens-are-alarming-heres-how-parents-can-change-that/?nor.

12   Lambda Legal, "Working with homeless LGBTQ youth," Lambda Legal, https://www.lambdalegal.org/know-your-rights/article/youth-homeless.

13   *UChicago News*, "LGBTQ young adults experience homelessness at more than twice the rate of their peers," April 27, 2018, https://news.uchicago.edu/story/lgbtq-young-adults-experience-homelessness-more-twice-rate-their-peers.

14   "Suicide and Violence Prevention," Centers for Disease Control, https://www.cdc.gov.gov/msmhealth/suicide-violence-prevention.htm.

15   S.E. James, L.L. Herman, L. Rankin, M. Keisling, L. Mottet, and M. Anafi, "The Report of the 2015 U.S. Transgender Survey," Washington, DC: National Center for Transgender Equality, 2016, https://transequality.org/sites/default/files/docs/usts/USTS-Full-Report-Dec17.pdf.

16   Brian S. Mustanski, PhD, corresponding author Robert Garofalo, MD, MPH, and Erin M. Emerson, MA, "Mental Health Disorders, Psychological Distress, and Suicidality in a Diverse Sample of Lesbian, Gay, Bisexual, and Transgender Youths," *American Journal of Public Health,* 100, no. 12 (2010): 2426-32, https://www.ncbi.nlm.nih.gov/pmc/articles/PMC2978194/.

17   Michael Kerr, "Depression in the LGBTQ+ Population," Healthline, July 8, 2016, https://www.healthline.com/health/depression/gay.

18   L. Kann, E.O. Olsen, T. McManus, et al., "Sexual Identity, Sex of Sexual Contacts, and Health-Related Behaviors Among Students in Grades 9-12—United States and Selected Sites, 2015," Morbidity and Mortality Weekly Report (MMWR), Centers for Disease Control and Prevention, Surveillance Summaries, August 12, 2016, https://www.cdc.gov/mmwr/volumes/65/ss/ss6509a1.htm.

19   Katy Steinmetz, "Why Transgender People are being murdered at a Historic Rate," Time, August 17, 2015, http://time.com/3999348/transgender-murders-2015/.

20   Lambda Legal, "Working with Homeless LGBTQ Youth," Lamba Legal, https://www.lambdalegal.org/know-your-rights/article/youth-homeless.

21   Kerith J. Conron, Shoshana K. Goldberg and Carolyn T. Halpern, "Socioeconomic Status of Sexual Minorities," Williams Institute, September 2018, https://williamsinstitute.law.ucla.edu/research/ses-sexual-minorities/.

22   Public Policy Office, "Sex and HIV Education," Guttmacher Institute, February 1, 2019, https://www.guttmacher.org/state-policy/explore/sex-and-hiv-education.

23   Jody L. Herman, PhD, Andrew R. Flores, PhD, Taylor N. T. Brown, MPP, Bianca D.M. Wilson, PhD, and Kerith J. Conron, ScD, "Age of Individuals Who Identify as Transgender in the United States," Williams Institute, January 17, 2017, https://williamsinstitute.law.ucla.edu/research/transgender-issues/new-estimates-show-that-150000-youth-ages-13-to-17-identify-as-transgender-in-the-us/.

24   Phillip L. Hammack, Ilan H. Meyer, Evan A. Krueger, Marguerita Lightfoot, and David M. Frost, "HIV Testing and PrEP Use in Different Generations of Gay and Bisexual Men," Williams Institute, September 2018, https://williamsinstitute.law.ucla.edu/research/hiv-and-prep/.

25   Caitlin Ryan, PhD, "Helping Families Support Their Lesbian, Gay, Bisexual, and Transgender (LGBT) Children," Washington, DC: National Center for Cultural Competence, Georgetown University Center for Child and Human Development, 2009, https://nccc.georgetown.edu/documents/LGBTQ+_Brief.pdf.

26   Sex Info Online, "Homosexuality and Religion," University of California Santa Barbara, February 17, 2017, http://www.soc.ucsb.edu/sexinfo/article/homosexuality-and-religion.

27   Ibid.

28   Ibid.

29   "Revised Standard Version," https://en.wikipedia.org/wiki/Revised_Standard_Version, citing: Daniel J. Harrington (1979), Interpreting the New Testament: A Practical Guide. Liturgical Press. pp. 26–ISBN 978-0-8146-5124-7.

Citing: *Michael David Coogan; Marc Zvi Brettler; Carol Ann Newsom; Pheme Perkins (2010). The New Oxford Annotated Bible: New Revised Standard Version: with the Apocrypha: an Ecumenical Study Bible. Oxford University Press. pp. 18–. ISBN 978-0-19-528955-8.*

30 Wikipedia, "Terminology of Homosexuality," https://en.wikipedia.org/wiki/Terminology_of_homosexuality.

31 Forge, "Has 'Homosexual' always been in the Bible?" March 21, 2019, https://www.forgeonline.org/blog/2019/3/8/what-about-romans-124-27.

32 Ibid.

33 Nicole LeFavour, "Top Ten Reasons Idaho Does Not Need a Religious Freedom Exemption to Add the Words," March 5, 2019, www.4idaho.org/tag/senator-brent-hill/

34 Ibid.

35 John McCrostie, "I'm a Lawyer and lawmaker. But because I'm gay, Idaho law doesn't protect my freedoms," *Idaho Statesman*, June 17, 2018, https://www.idahostatesman.com/opinion/readers-opinion/article213244924.html.

36 J.E. Hansan, "Jim Crow Laws and Racial Segregation," Virginia Commonwealth University Social Welfare History Project, 2011. Retrieved November 20, 2018, http://socialwelfare.library.vcu.edu/eras/civil-war-reconstruction/jim-crow-laws-andracial-segregation/.

37 Ibid.

38 Rupert W. Nacoste, PhD, *A Quiet Revolution*, April 9, 2016, https://www.psychologytoday.com/us/blog/quiet-revolution/201604/bathrooms-have-always-been-civil-rights-issue.

39 Ibid.

40 Gregory M. Herek, PhD, University of California-Davis, 1997-2012, http://psychology.ucdavis.edu/rainbow/html/military_history.html.

41 Rod Powers, "Policies Concerning LGBTQ People in the U.S. Military," May 31, 2018, https://www.thebalancecareers.com/policy-concerning-homosexuals-us-military-3347134.

42 Jennifer Hansler and Richard Roth, "US Halts Visas for Diplomats' Gay Partners," CNN, October 2, 2018, https://www.cnn.com/2018/10/02/politics/same-sex-couples-diplomatic-visas/index.html.

43   Trudy Ring, "Texas GOP Endorses 'Ex-Gay' Therapy, Hate-Crimes Law Repeal, Marriage Reversal," *The Advocate*, June 20, 2018, https://www.advocate.com/politics/2018/6/20/texas-gop-endorses-ex-gay-therapy-hate-crimes-law-repeal-marriage-reversal.

44   Caitlin Ryan, David Huebner, Rafael M. Diaz, Jorge Sanchez, "Family Rejection as a Predictor of Negative Health Outcomes in White and Latino Lesbian, Gay, and Bisexual Young Adults," Family Acceptance Project™, January 2009, *Pediatrics*, 123 no.1: 346-52, https://pediatrics.aappublications.org/content/123/1/346.

45   Michelle Bass, MSW, "LGBTQ+ Youth Transitioning Out of Foster Care," University of Victoria, Canada, 2011.

46   George Godwyn, Facebook post, October 21, 2018, https://www.facebook.com/permalink.php?story_fbid=2188822101397225&id=100008083698763.

47   History.com editors, "Stonewall Riots," August 21, 2018, http://www.history.com/topics/the-stonewall-riots.

48   Ibid.

49   Jason Marsden, "The Murder of Matthew Shepard," November 8, 2014, *WyoHistory*, https://www.wyohistory.org/encyclopedia/murder-matthew-shepard.

50   Nicole Blanchard, "Nampa man will plead guilty to hate crime in gay man's murder near Lake Lowell," *Idaho Statesman*, January 25, 2017, https://www.idahostatesman.com/news/local/crime/article128765204.html.

51   Anna Webb, "Lake Lowell beating death may energize Idaho gay rights movements," May 21, 2016 (updated May 23, 2016), *Idaho Statesman*, https://www.idahostatesman.com/news/politics-government/state-politics/article79095167.html.

52   Bryan Lyda, quoted by Anna Webb, Ibid., https://www.idahostatesman.com/news/politics-government/state-politics/article79095167.html

53   ACON, "In Pursuit of Truth & Justice," https://www.acon.org.au/wp-content/uploads/2018/05/In-Pursuit-of-Truth-and-Justice-Report-FINAL-220518.pdf.

54   Gary Nunn, "Gay-hating killers among us," *The Mercury*, December 3, 2017, https://www.themercury.com.au/rendezview/gayhating-killers-walk-among-us/news-story/c96dca891ac4404d5210f1b4749fe4b1.

55   Nelson Renteria, "'Am I next?': Killings in El Salvador leave transgender people in fear," *Reuters*, March 27, 2017, https://www.reuters.com/article/us-el-salvador-lgbt-violence-idUSKBN16Z1QR.

56   Ibid.

57   NoStringsNG, "Here's a list of countries where gay people are executed," February 14, 2019, https://nostringsng.com/list-gay-countries-executed/.

58   Lambda Legal, "Working with Homeless LGBTQ Youth," Lambda Legal, https://www.lambdalegal.org/know-your-rights/article/youth-homeless.

59   Ask the Expert, "Tips for Parents of LGBT Youth," https://www.hopkinsmedicine.org/health/articles-and-answers/ask-the-expert/tips-for-parents-lgbtq-youth.

60   Ibid.

61   Ibid.